This Place
A Texas Perspective
A Collection Edited By
JOYCE GIBSON ROACH

University of North Texas Press

© 1992 University of North Texas Press

All Rights Reserved
Printed in the United States of America

10 9 8 7 6 5 4 3 2 1

Requests for permission to reproduce material from this work
should be sent to:

Permissions
University of North Texas Press
Post Office Box 13856
Denton, Texas 76203

The paper in this book meets the minimum requirements of the
American National Standard for Permanence of Paper for Printed
Library Materials, z39.48-1984.

Library of Congress Cataloging-in-Publication Data

This place of memory : a Texas perspective : a collection / edited
by Joyce Gibson Roach.
        p.   cm.
  Includes bibliographical references.
  ISBN 0-929398-32-7
  1. Texas—Literary collections. 2. American literature—
  Texas.
I. Roach, Joyce Gibson.
PS558.T4T46   1992
810.8'032764—dc20   92-6890
                                            CIP

This Place of Memory is dedicated to the Texas Committee for the Humanities, and the Texas Folklore Society who, through their work, conserve the best of Texas, past and present, for the future—the 21st Century!

Acknowledgment and thanks are offered for the following pieces:

"Inner-City Scene: Fort Worth," Betsy Colquitt, from *Concho River Review*, Spring 1990.
"Toward An Understanding of Place for Southwestern Indians," Jane Young, from *New Mexico Folklore Record* 16. 1987:1-13.
"Who," "Football," Tim Seibles, from *Body Moves*, San Antonio: Corona Press, 1988.
"Nomenclature," Ernest Speck, from *An Assortment of Effusions*, Hobbs: Hawk Press, 1989.
"Remembrances from Childhood," Lionel Garcia, from *Houston Chronicle, Texas Magazine*, August 18, 1989.
"Aunt-Irene-and-Uncle-George," Jan Seale, from *New American*, Vol.4. No.3, 1982.
"Traditions," Neil Daniel, from *Fort Worth Star-Telegram*, July 3, 1984; "Over the Fence," "Sidewalks" from the Ryan Place Newsletter.
"The Day Gene Went Up Against Bambi," Tony Clark, from *Llano Sons: Three From the Southwest*, Hobbs: La Prinsa, 1976. "The Devil in Fort Worth," from *Llano Sons: Trips and Passings*, Hobbs: Hawk Press, 1989.
"Mary, This Place," "There Is No Day Better Than This," Jim Harris from *Stalking Place*, Hobbs: Hawk Press, 1988.

Grateful acknowledgment is made to Betsy Colquitt for suggesting the quotation from Katherine Anne Porter's *Noon Wine* as a title for the book, to Charlotte Wright for editorial guidance and assistance, to Kate Lynass for help of all kinds, and to Fran Vick for thinking of the book in the first place and for opening doors which seemed to be stuck.

Book design and illustrations
by Charles Shaw

CONTENTS

INTRODUCTION
"*Every Man Needs a Heath*," xi

TERRITORY

ELMER KELTON
What's Wrong With Being Different?, 4

MARGARET RAMBIE
Strong Land, Strong Cattle, 11

JANE YOUNG
Toward An Understanding of Place for the Southwestern Indians, 18

ERNEST SPECK
Nomenclature, 25

PAUL PATTERSON
Sometimes I Get Lonesome for Lonesome, 27

RED STEAGALL
To An Old Friend, 34
The Memories in Grandmother's Trunk, 37

CLAY REYNOLDS
New York, New York, 39

NEIGHBORHOOD

NEIL DANIEL
Neighborhood, 48

BETSY COLQUITT
Inner-City Scene: Ft. Worth, 54

DUANE BIDWELL
Where the Buddha Dwells, 60

JAN SEALE
Aunt-Irene-and-Uncle-George, 65

JOYCE ROACH
The Best Time, 69

SHELTERS

ERNESTINE SEWELL
. . . in the Kitchen, 78

PAUL K. CONNER
The Office, 86

JAMES WARD LEE
Tubby's Trailer, 91

TONY CLARK
The Day Gene Went Up Against Bambi, 102
The Devil in Fort Worth, Texas, 104

FRANCES MAYHUGH HOLDEN
Kaleidoscope, 107

EVERETT FLY
Landscape, Buildings & a Sense of Place, 110

RITUALS

JUDY ALTER
Fool Girl, 114

JIM HARRIS
Mary, This Place, 120
There Is No Day Better Than This, 122

ROBERT FLYNN
Women Don't Know, 123

TIM SEIBLES
Who, 130
Nothing But Football, 132

F. E. ABERNETHY
Sweet August, 135

LIONEL GARCIA
Remembrances of Childhood, 141

ROBERT COMPTON
A Bibliography of Place, 146

CONTRIBUTORS, 152

"... This place of memory is filled with landscapes shimmering in light and color, moving with sounds and shapes."

Noon Wine
Katherine Anne Porter

Introduction

"Every man needs a heath"

*E*verybody's got a place or wants one. Even history needs a place. Since before recorded time, history has often hung on some place, some territory, that somebody else wanted. In Texas more than 150 years ago, men of many places and persuasions and for various reasons wanted the Alamo, or at least what the place represented. The Alamo—the place rejected and decaying but waiting through the years, catching and holding the liquids of the frontier cultural metaphor in the stone vessel of the chapel until the significance poured over the walls and spilled into a new republic. Now, the word alone suffices for place; *the* place by which we Texans measure ourselves, history, politics, literature, folklore, philosophy, or at least we used to.

But place is more personal. Every man and woman needs their own space. Harry Ransom, in a preface to *Texian Stompin' Grounds*, a volume of the Texas Folklore Society, put it this way:

> Among the feelings that have moved men powerfully, none has been more universal than love of the earth. Consciously or unconsciously, silently or in defiant proclamations, men have always identified themselves with their native soil. With their own countryside, with their home rock, they have associated the forces of their lives. Young men, not always in vain, have died for this ideal of the land; poets have sung it and old men have celebrated it in story. It has made some men narrow, but it has made others heroic. Famed or nameless, each of us is moved by this feeling for the place of his growth. Every man deserves a native heath.

In 1941, when Ransom wrote, America stood on the front side of war not knowing what would be on the backside, and fifty years later, we can affirm Ransom's philosophy because the world has stood close to the very same place once again. We can add that every person deserves at the very least a sense of place, of belonging, that may defy mere location; a feeling that is portable and may be transported into harm's way on someone else's dry ground.

The words, sense of place, have a familiar ring to most of us who are forty-something even if we can't define the words exactly. We have a general idea about what the words mean. Such a phrase conjures pleasant feelings and memories, provides an aura of well being about home or the home-place in a particular geographical locale, or in the memory of it. While everybody ought to have a place, the same phrase is unfamiliar, even peculiar, to many of the Pepsi Generation, whoever they are, and even they don't seem to know. At least we middle-aged-to-older-to-downright-elderly know who we are and a sense of place seems to have something to do with the knowing. In many ways those of us who grew up in the fifties were the last faces on a Norman Rockwell painting, the last innocents, the last believers. After that generation, mankind made the greatest strides away from innocence and a good deal more.

Ultra moderns have the impression that they can buy whatever they don't have or at least it is a worthy aim to pursue the means to buy. Along with material pursuit, there appears to be a longing, a yearning, a vague sensation of something missing, a sense of not having a place but of being able to create or find it as they go—the Mobile Society, it is called.

Psychologists and others in charge by profession of observing and treating mankind's mental condition, notice that today's folk seem afraid out of all proportion of the feeling of loneliness, of being alone, of no sensation of place. Groups for recreation, similar interests, education, therapy, meditation and worship offer a place to fit in, to find one's self, to go to. Bumper stickers and T shirt messages do a large business in telling us who we are and how good we are at it.

But this is also the era of the return to nostalgia as if a return is therapeutic. Restauranteurs, clothiers, interior designers, crafters grasp the past and offer it as visible evidence of things not seen, offer it like a talisman. The offerings evoke a sense of place, belonging, sanctuary. Small town, rural places featuring stereotypical characters in that setting are "in" in the publishing world, in the visual world of TV and movies. Historical societies, museums, exhibits featuring old timey life are popular. Plays and music of the past are finding new audiences. Neighborhood life in cities is becoming important again. Architects whether in housing developments or shopping centers offer styles of the past even if cost is modern. Fashion designers look back not forward and remind the wearer of being in the costume of a certain period. Could it be that the renaissance of the past has to do with trying to capture and hold on to someone else's sense of place in a world that has none?

This generation has been identified by politicians, anthropologists and psychiatrists as the Displaced, Disenfranchised, Lost, Hopeless, Homeless, Factually Overloaded, Disinherited—labels that suggest where their feelings of place are. Sense of place lacks definition and recognition except in negative terms. The hearth, the heath, the rock, *a donde nos juntamos*, the fire pit, the kitchen—all are disappearing. The home is changing. And not just in our own country. Refugees all over the world from Africa to Asia, from South America to Russia, from Iraq to the streets of Houston, Texas are wandering, children and belongings on their backs. The reasons for the exodus are easy to spot. The Four Horsemen are the cause, of course, regardless of whose country's horses they ride or whose racing colors they wear.

We, as citizens of the world, are great noticers of things after the fact but we are provided with daily TV coverage complete with pictures to help us become expert witnesses. Regardless of the cause for wandering anywhere on planet Earth, I believe that every race is, in one way or another, trying to find the kitchen again, the hearth, a place to stop and prepare something to eat for spirit as well as body not only for themselves but for those called family. We are all searching for that place of belonging, of safety, of place; that locale where survival instincts and basic needs are fulfilled in a location that smells, yea verily, reeks of sanctuary because we hunger, figuratively and literally, for place.

It would be hard not to notice that more words have been

devoted to describing the absence or loss of sense of place without ever quite defining the phrase. We know more about what it isn't than what it is; more about who doesn't have it than who does. It is time to get to the heart of the matter, to offer a meaning and definition of a sense of place from those who remember in order to remind those who have forgotten or don't know, may never know; time to offer a recording that perhaps may even serve as a guide as Texans approach the threshold of the twenty-first century.

Directing the question, "What does sense of place mean to you?" to the writers and thinkers across the state, one might suppose that their contributions would deal with what A.C. Greene and other literary giants refer to as personal country. To be sure that place of growing up, the home country, is central still to many. Polling the contributors, however, revealed a surprising and rich variety of designations. Some said sense of place was in their work, in art, in photography, in performance, in religion, in preserving the past, in people, in words and names, in medicine, in the arms of the beloved, in the creative life, in architecture, in feelings even. Place had to do with sounds, smells, tastes. The volume is double edged because sense of place was squarely in the written work in all its forms—witty, scholarly, popular, serious—fiction, essay, poem, reminiscence, newspaper reporting, scholarly treatise. Writing about sense of place had to do with city dwellers and small town dwellers; desert or beside the gulf stream water dwellers; plains or prairie or piney woods dwellers. Telling had to do as well with ethnicity, and of being male or female.

While sense of place was something different for each of the contributors, it was possible to come up with a general consensus about the phrase. It certainly had to do with location and everything to do with where a person was most comfortable with himself and herself, most balanced. In every case the sense of place was personal and not a group experience, an individual expression of completeness, a solitary experience even if a certain group played a part in the activity. Sense of place could always be attached to location even if the location was inside one's own mind. It was always knowing beyond a shadow of a doubt that one was complete, satisfied, not wanting, not needing and that even if sense of place was occasionally fleeting, it served as a point of reference, of return and it was always there to call on, to summon, to sustain, and to find again.

We Texans have ever been ones to identify what was important and spend lots of money on museums and displays and studies telling about what we have lost. It is easier and much less costly than trying to reverse the losing. Texas is a fortunate state to have so many ready to preserve the past while keeping a finger on the pulse of the present and the future. But we are also more than fortunate in having those who capture in writing the works which preserve not only things, places and people but the feelings about them. Preserving both in words and in visible evidence demands that we learn something, be reminded of a truth that will be valuable in the future.

This Place of Memory is a broad statement for the humanities, an affirmation that Texas will carry much of the best into the future and will find not a strange and alien century, but one built on the familiar because we still have a sense of place, if simply places in the heart. We have only to call the best of Texas' past from the kingdoms of the minds of the contributors to see how sturdy the link to the future where yet another harbor, another sanctuary, lies waiting to be discovered by other generations because something about the new place and time is familiar. Every man and woman will always deserve a heath by whatever name he or she chooses to call it, wherever it may be.

—JOYCE GIBSON ROACH

TERRITORY

Nothing speaks louder of sense of place in Texas than territory, breadth and width, height and depth, from Texarkana to El Paso, Amarillo to Brownsville. **Elmer Kelton** *tells just how wide, deep and long place is and how each geographical division marks and distinguishes those who live there.* **Margaret Rambie** *writes of Arturo Alonzo who cannot define sense of place in words, but knows that it has something to do with red cattle and strong land, and that both have dictated the course of his life.* **Jane Young** *offers the anthropologist's view. She speaks of pueblo and desert dwellers rather than just Texas Indians, recognizing that natives did not count the Rio Grande or the Red as boundaries to their territories. In writing of the Indians in the Southwest, especially the Zuni and Cibeque Apaches, she speaks of a similar group like the Tiqua near Ysleta in Far West Texas who share a common cultural perspective. In 1836, part of New Mexico was also part of the Texas Republic. Included is an extensive bibliography for those who wish to read more.* **Ernest Speck** *echoes in poetry Young's idea that place names are vital to place and cannot exist without them.* **Paul Patterson** *offers the philosophy that living in harsh country marked his feelings in such a way that sometimes he gets "lonesome for lonesome"—the Trans-Pecos region of Texas.* **Clay Reynolds**, *in an excerpt from a novel in progress,* Texas Augustus, *addresses the problem of territorial names from the perspective of a Texan transplanted to New York City.* **Red Steagall**, *the cowboy poet laureate for the state of Texas, who both sings and speaks of the cattle range, knows that era is gone but reminds Westerners of the values of the past. In the traditional form and style of cowboy poetry, Red takes the reader not to the branding fire, but rather to a rest home where an old man recreates his territory from memory, or into a trunk where a woman's place is stored.*

What's Wrong With Being Different?

ELMER KELTON

*T*exans have an old adage: if you don't like the weather, wait thirty minutes and it will change. A variation on this could be: if you don't like it where you are, drive fifty miles and it will be different.

Ours is a highly diverse state, more so than most people recognize if they have not traveled, lived and worked in several parts of it. This diversity is a frustration to those who would try to characterize Texas in a simplistic way. It is a frustration to writers—especially outsiders—who want to sum up the whole meaning of the state in one essay or even one book.

El Paso is not like Texarkana. Dallas is vastly different in tone and outlook from Fort Worth despite the proximity of those two cities, tied together as they are in what today is being called the "metroplex," as if they were clones sharing one cookie sheet. Amarillo and Brownsville are not the same, nor should they ever want to be.

A professor who grew up in a distant Western state was surprised, even after teaching in Texas for several years, when I pointed out to her that Texas is divided into a number of distinct geographical regions including the blacklands, the piney woods, the upper and lower Gulf coasts, the Rio Grande Valley, the Rio Grande Prairie, the Hill Country, the Cross Timbers, the Rolling, Lower and High Plains, the Edwards Plateau, the Trans-Pecos. Each of these areas differs from the others in topography, vegetation, climate and, to some degree, people.

This diversity gives each of us a sense of being from a place that has a unique personality, duplicated nowhere. That place marks each of us as a product of it. No matter how far we may eventually wander, some of it lingers with us, coloring our perceptions of the world.

My own heritage is the ranching and oilpatch country of West Texas, near the Pecos River. To the stranger, it can be a harsh and forbidding land where summer heat sets the horizon line to wriggling like a snake, where green grass is scarce and most forms of vegetation come armed for protection with thorns that seem to jump out and stab you. But growing up there, I took all this in stride and was only vaguely aware that other parts of the state were vastly different. If nature was stingy with her blessings, scarcity taught us to appreciate those blessings more—those and any others which came our way in later years and in other places.

My work as an agricultural writer has taken me to just about all parts of Texas and has given me an appreciation for the unique assets which each section offers.

To many people who have gained their impressions of Texas mostly from Hollywood, the icon often is a cowboy—an Anglo cowboy at that—riding horseback across a desert amid tall cactus and bleached cattle skulls. Maybe—just maybe—an oil derrick stands on the horizon. That is a far cry from the reality of the Brazos River bottoms in Central Texas, where cottonfields alternate with milo maize, and where stocker cattle spend the winter grazing open fields of lush green wheat and oats. The men found working cattle there are as likely to be black or Hispanic as Anglo. The image does not quite fit the reality of the South Texas brush country either, where the prickly pear may grow head high to a tall cowboy, but that cowboy will usually be Hispanic. The image is a far cry from the ricefields along the Gulf Coast, the dark woods of deep East Texas or the citrus groves of the Lower

Rio Grande Valley. And how many cowboy hats are you likely to see in downtown Dallas?

One obvious point of difference across the state is weather. An old rule of thumb says that as you move westward from Texarkana you lose about an inch of rainfall per year for each fifty miles. That doesn't work out one hundred percent, but the principle has some validity. This difference in precipitation has a direct effect upon the vegetation native to each area. Deep East Texas may grow tall green grass, lush to look at but so empty of nutrition that a cow can starve standing belly-deep in it unless she is given supplemental protein. In far West Texas, nature over thousands of years has culled the native grasses to those species that can stand prolonged periods of drought, that can break out of the bare, parched ground and produce a seed crop for its perpetuation on a one-inch rain. Moreover, that grass is likely to be rich in nutrition. It seems that the more the difficulty, the stronger the grass.

That goes for people, too. Those who live in a rain-shy land of perpetual challenge seem to grow tougher, more resilient and more resolute. Dr. Walter Prescott Webb pointed out that the land changes character west of the 98th meridian, and so do the people who live there, especially if they must make their living directly from the land as ranchers or farmers, facing the constant challenge of too little rain, too many natural obstacles.

For those readers who don't know where the meridian lies, Interstate 35 is a workable substitute. There are places along the north-south highway where you can almost perceive the difference between the two sides of the underpass. On the east side, more often than not, the vegetation will be green. On the west, it will tend toward the dry, much of the time desperately so.

To the east lie Dallas and the blacklands, the piney woods, Aggieland and Houston. To the west lie often-dusty ranching and farming country, the Permian Basin oilfields, the beautiful limestone outcrops of the Hill Country and the Edwards Plateau, the chaparral and thick brush of the borderland.

There are palpable differences in the people, at least in their reactions to other people and the world around them. A majority of Texans live east of I-35. People there are plentiful—overplentiful, some would declare—and folks commonly pay little attention to anybody else on the sidewalk or on the street unless they see an overt threat. West of I-35, however, passing motorists on the two-land roads are likely to give you a tentative wave, or at least an uplifted two or three fingers as a friendly gesture. On long, open highways where traffic is thin, it is almost as if they are glad to see someone else alive.

When I first went to the University of Texas back in 1942, a green kid from the West Texas sandhills, I would nod at people I passed on campus and along the Drag. I quickly found that those who did not react with surprise and suspicion were likely to be small-town or country students, most often from the western part of the state where Western hospitality remains alive if not always well, even today. Students from Dallas and Houston probably thought I was about to put the touch on them for something, and they would quickly treat me to the averted gaze.

The sparser the population, the more friends and neighbors are treasured, and the more welcome strangers are made to feel. This probably is a carryover from the early generations of Texas settlement when neighbors were few and company scarce. There was a time, and it lasted through at least the early years of the automobile age, when it was bad manners to pass a farm or ranch house without stopping to visit, break bread and, if it was late in the day, to "stay all night."

There are some who regard rural customs as being hopelessly outmoded in this increasingly urban age, when architects, city planners and national chains seem hell-bent on making everything look alike, in erasing the marks of distinction between one city and another.

A prominent Texas writer declared a few years ago that Texas has become an urban state, and that any author who wants to write with validity about modern Texas must write about urban life. He indicated that small-town and rural experience is no longer relevant. But that viewpoint ignores the fact of the great rural land mass west of I-35 and the people—admittedly a numerical minority—who still live there.

Take a Texas roadmap and cut out the yellow parts that represent the major cities: Dallas, Fort Worth, Houston, San Antonio, Austin. It won't change the picture much to add El Paso, Corpus Christi and Waco, and even Amarillo and Lubbock. Lay all these down over the Big Bend National Park. They will barely more than cover the park; they won't begin to fill Brewster County.

Texas' huge rural land area and the people who live on it, away from the major urban centers, are by no means irrelevant. True, they no longer have great political power except when they manage to be a swing vote, but they remain a potent influence.

Those cities do not exist in a vacuum. A great many of the people who cluster in them because of work or other considerations have come from the small towns and cities, or from the country, bringing with them the lessons and attitudes of that rural upbringing. One reared in Jacksboro or Andrews or George West does not shed the old values at the city limits of Houston or Dallas or San Antonio. Past experience carries its influence forward and colors the new surroundings for better or worse.

Even so, the city imposes its own attitudes, and the old influences diminish with each succeeding generation that is not firmly rooted to the place of its forebears.

In my earliest years I thought the whole world must be cattle, horses and cowboys, because that was about all I ever saw, that and a forest of tall wooden oil derricks standing in the distance. My father was a cowboy and later a foreman on a large ranch at the edge of the Crane–Upton County oilpatch. At the time it seemed to me that the ranch and the oilfield were two different worlds. As I grew older I came to realize that the people in those two worlds were more alike than different, for a great many came from the same rootstock. All of them left their mark on me, a sense of belonging to a definite place and a unique class of people. I revere them, warts and all.

The cowboys were my first big influence. As a group they could be kind and merciless, both at the same time. They were tolerant teachers so long as you gave them an honest effort, but they could make life miserable if they sensed that you were dogging it. They had a keen-eyed way of seeing through pretense, of shucking the corn right down to the cob. They delighted especially in humiliating the braggart, impaling him on his own brass horn. To this day I have a hard time with self-promotion, remembering the treatment those cowpunchers meted out to anyone who saw more in the mirror than they thought was there.

Probably a majority of the oilfield folk I knew as a boy had come from farms, ranches and small towns, so their outlook was not unlike that of my own family elders. That they were caught up at sixty miles an hour in a whole new world did not erase the values—and the prejudices—they had brought with them. Oilfield tradition tends to emphasize the violent and bawdy aspects of the boomtowns, but a great many of the early oilfielders were extremely devout. Even as a boy I sensed the sharp dichotomy between the holy-rollers and the hell-rollers who shared that community. Parental and school influences being what they were, I saw a lot more of the former than of the latter, and I still carry much of their twig-bending influence.

After these many years, the smell and sound of a honkytonk or club still make me feel uneasy and arouse a vague and probably unjustified sense of guilt for even considering going in. I can never travel far enough to get completely away from those strong-minded oilpatch folks of my youth. Often, called upon to make a judgment, I catch myself wondering what *they* would have thought, and thinking likewise.

Wherever I go, a little of Crane, my sandhills home place, goes with me.

We all need this anchor, this assurance of knowing who we are and where we come from, this sense of place or home country that the Mexican people call *querencia*. For each of us it is different. For each of us it is special.

One of the saddest developments of recent times, to me, has been the gradual draining of population from the countryside and the small towns, once the beating heart of the state. The exodus to major urban centers has been an economic boon to the cities, of course, and they all want to keep growing larger no matter how severe the problems of serving this growth. But the cost has been high to the traditions and the atmosphere which have given each part of the state, each locality, a personality of its own. Modern urbanization inevitably brings a degree of amalgamation, an assembly-line sameness, a loss of individual identity and, ultimately, a loss of this strong sense of place.

Walk into the average urban mall and you'll search in vain for any distinctive flavor of the community. Usually you can't tell whether you are in Cape Cod or Hickory Bend.

I dread the day that we may step out into the sunlight and still not be able to tell where we are.

Photos by L. K. Travis

Strong Land, Strong Cattle

MARGARET RAMBIE

"When quail get together and start talking, it's a good sign it's going to rain. When it's dry you won't see but one or two running together. Yesterday I saw about 20 crossing the road, just like those up ahead," Arturo Alonzo said pointing to a covey scurrying across the Chaparrosa Ranch road just ahead of the pickup.

"The *cenizo* is blooming. Some people say that means rain. I hope so. We need it. This country comes back fast after a rain," he said shaking his head at grass turning brown in pastures. "At least we have the brush."

Cattle manager for B. K. Johnson, Arturo worked at Johnson's 65,000 acre Chaparrosa Ranch but lives nearby on the Mangum Ranch. Both are deep in the heart of the arid Southwest Texas brush country near La Pryor.

"We have a drought about every seven years that lasts about three. Back in the 50s, I thought it would never rain again. I still remember when that drought broke. It rained 12 inches in an hour. This one has a while to go, but the cattle are doing pretty good.

We've had more rain than some places," he said, stopping at the El Paso pasture gate.

"The pasture's named like the town in West Texas," he said. "The El Paso pasture is right next to the Gaviota. All the pastures have names."

Arturo opened the gate, pulled the pickup into El Paso and then got out and walked through the herd, checking the cows and calves, jotting down ear-tag numbers on the palm of his hand.

"They look pretty good," he said as the animals crowded around him. "Of course, we're feeding some now. I heard about a ranch where they were hauling water to cattle. You're in trouble when you start hauling water. If you run out of water, sell. You can substitute for the grass, but there is no substitute for water."

Arturo will talk about red cattle, the weather, his seven children, of his fourteen grandchildren, but try to start him talking about himself and the words get as sparse as the rain that seldom falls on the brush country where he has lived and worked for over 40 years.

Ask him about the Santa Gertrudis cattle he has fitted and shown for almost 30 of those 40 years and he'll smile and tell you about bulls named Masterpiece and Senor Pico and about winning championships at stock shows from Houston to St. Louis. Then ask him about the mesquite and prickly pear dotted territory where the red cattle thrive and he'll smile again and tell you about country that is strong even when it's dry, that has soil so filled with nutrients that cattle stay fat just eating the brush.

But ask Arturo about his "sense of place" and the smile disappears. The phrase is foreign to him, even puzzling. He has never thought about a "sense of place," he says.

Place is where he lives, works with red cattle. Ask him to define place and he talks about the cattle country he loves. To know it is to know Arturo. He belongs in and to and around and about the South Texas brush country.

Like the plants that thrive there, Arturo's roots run deep, reaching down for whatever is needed to survive on the strip of land that lies between the Rio Grande and Nueces rivers. A strip of land early settlers called harsh, pony soldiers called hell, Easterners still call ugly and Arturo calls strong.

"It may not look it but this is strong country, even in a drought. In east Texas or Louisiana it needs to rain every other day to have fat cattle. If it doesn't rain, the cattle go to hell. Here the cattle can eat brush and stay fat. This is cattle country, " he said.

Arturo knows cattle. He is one of the top Santa Gertrudis herdsmen in the United States. An intuitive geneticist, Arturo first encountered the red cattle that are 5/8 Shorthorn and 3/8 Brahman on the late C. A. McDaniel's Mirasol Ranch in 1960.

The encounter changed Arturo's life forever.

"I had seen some red cattle before when I worked in Mexico on a ranch near Musquiz, where I was born. But they weren't pure Santa Gertrudis. It was at the Mirasol that I first started with show cattle.

"When I moved to the Mirasol, I didn't know a thing about registered cattle. Show cattle are different from ranch cattle. I started my own breeding program, doing things my way. People liked my product. I have been breeding show cattle for 27 years," Arturo said.

Word about his natural ability to fit and show registered cattle spread. Other Santa Gertrudis breeders tried to lure him away from the Mirasol and then from the Chaparrosa Ranch where he began working in 1973, after Johnson bought the Mirasol herd.

"One man wanted me to go to Florida. But I didn't like it. Southwest Texas is my place. I didn't want to move 1,000 miles from here. The country there is no good.

"I have seen this country when the ground was so hard and bare you could play marbles on it. Get one good rain and the grass is back. I'm glad I didn't go to Florida. That ranch isn't around anymore. This country lasts."

It was 1941 and Arturo was 19 when he left his wife in Mexico and headed north with his brother Juan, looking for a better life. Somewhere along the way, although he would never call it such a thing, Arturo discovered a sense of place.

After a year in Normandy, near Ozona, Arturo made his way to Uvalde, a town closer to Mexico and to the wife he had left behind.

"The country around Uvalde is a lot like where I was born except there I was close to the Sierra Madre mountains. It is pretty there, especially in the morning. Here there are no mountains," he said looking out across mesquite flats whose name describes both the lay of the land and its vegetation.

"When I left Mexico, I was looking for a better life, but I never intended to stay in Texas. I might not have stayed if it hadn't been for Mr. Bob Ingram," he remembered.

"I went to work for Mr. Bob near Uvalde after Juan and I worked for two weeks digging rocks that were used in a house that was being built on Uvalde's main street. Whenever I drive by that house, I point it out to my wife, Concha and say, 'that house it still here and those rocks I dug. It is hard to believe, so much has happened since then.'

"I remember digging those rocks. It was in July and it was hot. I was glad to go to work for Mr. Bob. He helped me bring Concha and our children over.

"Mr. Bob's place was on the Nueces River. I was there for 11 years. Then I moved to the Mirasol Ranch. It was on the river too. I can't get away from the river. Now Concha and I live on the Mangum Ranch. The river runs through it, too, except it looks like a canal.

"I've seen the river run full and I've seen it dry. I can remember during the drought in 1955 when it either rained heavy up river or a dam broke and the water came down the Nueces. I watched it. There was a huge cloud of dust coming down the river in front of the water and there wasn't a drop of rain. It was strange," Arturo remembered.

"It happened on September 17. I'm sure. My daughter was born on September 16, *Diez y Seis* and the river came down the next day."

Arturo didn't move to the Mirasol—the name means sunflower—until 1960, four years after the infamous 50s drought ended.

The family lived there until 1982, when they moved to the Magnum Ranch.

Concha, Arturo and their three Mexico-born children became American citizens in 1970, the same year that the La Raza Unida party became a force in Mexican-American politics in South Texas, fostering school walkouts in Crystal City and Uvalde and causing an Anglo flight out of Crystal City. Arturo weathered the South Texas political storms of the 70s, just as he weathers nature's storms, by tending to business.

"We all went together and became American citizens. This is home, I would never go back," he said. "I'm not a native Texan but I love this state. I love this country. It has been good for me and for my family. When I left Musquiz I never dreamed I would do what I have done."

The things he has done include winning championships at every major fat stock show in the United States. He is such an excellent fitter and showman that he was made an honorary vice-president of the Texas State Fair Association. In 1982, Arturo was recognized by the Uvalde Chamber of Commerce. He was named Man of the Year in Agriculture.

"That was a surprise," he said shyly, handing over a newspaper article about that honor and another article about him that had appeared in the *Cattleman* magazine. Both had been decoupaged into wall plaques by his daughters.

At the Mirasol, Arturo began youth days and heifer sales that attracted 4-H and FFA members from across the state. He quietly advised young cattle breeders as they selected the calves they would raise for junior livestock shows like the Uvalde County's where he has worked as an advisor for years and where his sons walked away with championships of their own but then chose not to follow further in their father's footsteps.

"My oldest boy, Arturo, has a doctorate degree from Texas A&M and is in administration there. Juan and Lupe also graduated from A&M. Juan is a captain in the Marines. He will make a career of that.

"Lupe worked on Mr. Johnson's ranch at Carmel, California. He worked with horses. That amazed me. He understands horses like I understand cattle."

Then the ranch sold and now Lupe has a western and feed store. The girls all graduated from high school in Uvalde and soon went on to college. Arturo's oldest daughter, Concha, is married and works at the First State Bank in Uvalde. Soccoro is married and lives in California. Gloria lives in Ft. Worth and 28-year-old Dora lives at home with her parents and teaches school in La Pryor.

"I guess it has been a little disappointment that the boys didn't choose my work. I took them with me whenever I could when they were younger, but they must go their own way. Things are changing. Many of my grandchildren don't even speak Spanish and that is a shame. They are going to need it.

"My granddaughter did celebrate her *quinceanera* though. So all the customs aren't dying. But things are definitely changing," he said.

Recently, someone asked Arturo if he ever thought he would have a breeding program on a computer.

"Of course I didn't think that. Why would I?" he shrugged. "They didn't have computers when I started at the Mirasol. When I started working cattle in Mexico they didn't have chutes or pens, either."

While computers can do a lot of things, Arturo doesn't think they will ever replace a natural ability to know what cow to breed to what bull to get the best calf.

"It's good to keep track of things with the computer but I don't see any reason to change anything I have been doing for years," he said sitting in Chaparrosa Ranch headquarters surrounded by trophies won by and pictures of the championship cattle he fitted.

Arturo didn't need a computer to tell him to use the weather rather than fight it.

"Our breeding season is February through July so the babies will be born November through April. No summer calf, the heat is too hard on a baby.

"Some years back we started breeding for a slightly smaller cow. Not long ago, Texas A&M put out a paper that said the biggest cows were not the best producers. I knew that a long time ago. It didn't take research for me to know that big cows don't do good on a ranch. I just been breeding things my own way.

"I love the cattle. I'm proud of them. I helped myself learn about breeding. I crossed different ways until I got what I wanted.

"Masterpiece really did it. He is still in business after 19 years. We still have some of his semen stored, collected in the old way, in glass vials, not straws. It all started with Masterpiece," he said.

The bull that made the Mirasol Ranch famous and changed Arturo's life was five months old when the Alonzo family moved down river to the ranch. Another prize bull, Senor Pico, was born in 1968. Arturo used the two superior bulls to produce one of the best show strings of Santa Gertrudis cattle in the country.

Although the Chaparrosa Ranch no longer has a string of show cattle, Arturo actively managed the ranch's 3,500 head of

Santa Gertrudis and crossbred cattle. For years each November, buyers from the United States and Mexico came to the ranch for the Cowman's Choice Sale, buying cows, calves and bulls from Masterpiece and Senor Pico bloodlines.

At the sales, Arturo was quietly everywhere. In the show ring, inside the pens checking the cattle and outside talking to buyers about bloodlines.

Not long ago a young cowboy asked Arturo why he was the boss of everything.

"Because I know what I'm doing," said the man who has been doing it for 30 years. Sometimes though, I wish I could just be a cowboy again, get off at 5 P.M. and not worry," he said then added quickly, "I'm still healthy. I don't want to sit down and do nothing."

"I have always done my work. It is so easy here, if you are responsible and work hard. My father taught me that. I don't understand people who have been living here for years and never did better themselves. I just don't understand. You work hard and I guess then someday you retire.

"When I was 20 or 30, I thought 60 was an old man. Now I am 60 and I don't feel old. I'm not sure about retiring. I don't think I'll do that. Concha and I bought a weekend house in Uvalde in 1972. She talks about adding on and living there when we retire.

"I'll try it. But never, never did I live in town, never," Arturo said, making a fist and softly hitting the table for emphasis.

"I may just have to get me a little place, a few acres or so, run some cattle on them. I don't know if I can be away from the cattle. I know I'd miss them," he said in a whisper.

"Mi gusto vivir en el rancho, trabajar con vacas y caballos, caminar por los tardes."

Toward an Understanding of "Place" for the Southwestern Indians*

M. JANE YOUNG

Although anthropologists and folklorists have gathered an abundance of ethnographic information on the Southwestern Indians, they have published surprisingly few studies that focus directly on these Native Americans' use of place names and their attitudes toward places. This lacuna is not, however, exclusive to studies of Native Americans, but, rather, characteristic of folkloric/anthropological inquiry in general. As Keith Basso suggests,

> ... the activity of placenaming—the actual use of toponyms in concrete instances of everyday speech has attracted little attention from linguists and ethnographers. Less often still has placenaming been investigated as a universal means—and, it could well turn out, a universally primary means—for *appropriating* physical environments. (Basso 1987:7)

---

*Excerpted from a longer article.

I do not wish to promote the stereotype that Native Americans were or are noble savages, or that all Indians see themselves as intricately and harmoniously linked with the natural world. It is necessary to do research with specific tribes and individuals within such tribes to avoid a pan-Indian or pan-tribal stance. Nevertheless, such research often reveals that most Native Americans do share a similar way of looking at the land and at themselves as part of that land. Taking a narrower focus, what I want to stress is the importance of particular places, and, consequently the names of those places, to Native Americans of the Southwest. These places encompass not only spatial existence, but a temporal dimension as well. They frequently include both the homeplace or places of important events described in oral tradition, and the time of myth, legend, and history, when significant events that inform present day world view were enacted. Surely the significance of specific places to Native Americans is revealed in the importance to them of reclaiming these places whenever possible. Recently, my Zuni colleagues were exuberant over the fact that the place in Arizona identified as Kachina Village had, through land claims legislation, been "returned" to the tribe. A sadder example is revealed by the continuing agony caused to the Native Americans involved in the Navajo-Hopi land dispute—in this complicated and confusing situation both groups identify with the same places and there is no easy resolution to their dilemma.

Although ethnographers may have overlooked the concept of place, it forms a central theme in contemporary Native American writing. For example, Leslie Marmon Silko of Languna Pueblo suggests that the Puebloans do not see the land as *landscape*, for that implies that one is exterior to or apart from the land—perhaps even passively looking on. Silko writes,

> Pueblo potters, and the creators of petroglyphs and oral narratives, never conceived of removing themselves from the earth and sky. So long as the human consciousness remains *within* the hills, canyons, cliffs, and the plants, clouds, and sky, the term landscape, as it has entered the English language is misleading. "A portion does not correctly describe the relationship between the human being and his or her surroundings. This

> assumes the viewer is somehow *outside* or *separate from* the territory he or she surveys. Viewers are as much a part of the landscape as the boulder they stand on. (Silko 1986:84)

Because they regard the land as a living being and themselves as part of this living being—according to Puebloan origin myths the people are born from the womb of Mother Earth—the Puebloans see themselves as having a responsibility for the land (Smith 1988). The Kiowa writer, N. Scott Momaday describes this responsibility as a matter of reciprocal appropriations which are characteristic of the Native American ethic with respect to the physical world, "appropriations in which man invests himself in the landscape, and at the same time incorporates the landscape into his most fundamental experience" (Momaday 1976:80).

Anyone who has seen the films produced by Navajo filmmakers as part of the project inspired by Sol Worth and John Adair perceives the visual and temporal importance of the land for the Navajo (Worth and Adair 1972). Whether the films are about weaving, silversmithing, or healing, much of the actual footage is taken up with sweeping views of the landscape (and, frequently, as part of that landscape, the sheep). Not only are these films a statement about the importance of the land, but they indicate a focus on *process* as well—we see an image of the land in the act of being.

It is this symbolic sense of the landscape that is explored by Keith Basso, an anthropologist whose recent scholarship does much to fill in the gap in our awareness of Native American attitudes toward the land. Basso says,

> Landscapes are available in symbolic terms . . . and so, chiefly through the manifold agencies of speech, they can be "detached" from their fixed spatial mooring and transformed into instruments of thought and vehicles of purposive behavior. Thus transformed, landscapes and the places that fill them become tools for the imagination, expressive means for accomplishing verbal deeds, and also, of course, eminently portable possessions to which individuals can maintain deep and abiding attachments regardless of where they travel. In

> these ways . . . men and women learn to *appropriate* their landscapes, to think and act "with" them as well as about and upon them, and to weave them with spoken words into the foundations of social life. (Basso 1987:7)

For the Cibeque Apache with whom Basso has worked for many years, this weaving is accomplished by reciting place-names to one's self, pointing out particular locations, and pronouncing their names and using those names to remind others of their moral commitment to their people and the land. As Mrs. Annie Peaches says: "The land is always stalking people. The land makes people live right. The land looks after us. The land looks after people" (Basso 1984:21). Mr. Benson Lewis adds that the naming makes it possible to *see* a place even when one is far away from it. He says: "Elsewhere, hearing that mountain's name, I see it. Its name is like a picture. Stories go to work on you like arrows. Stories make you live right. Stories make you replace yourself" (Basso 1984:21). Basso concludes that,

> Place-names are used in all forms of Apache storytelling as situating devices, as conventionalized instruments for locating narrated events in the physical settings where the events have occurred. Thus, instead of describing these settings discursively, an Apache storyteller can simply employ their names and Apache listeners, whether they have visited the locations or not, are able to imagine in some detail how they might appear. In this way . . . narrated events are "spatially anchored" at points on the land, the evocative pictures presented by Western Apache place-names become indispensable resources for the storyteller's craft. (Basso 1984:32)

The examples Basso cites are highly descriptive, such as the Cibeque Apache place names that translate, "water flows inward underneath a cottonwood tree," or "water flows downward on top of a series of flat rocks" (Basso 1984:27). I would add that these points on the land can thus be taken as metonyms of narrative, evoking not just the image of the place names, but the emotions, the moral values, the stories associated with such places as well.

References Cited

Anaya, Rudolfo A. 1972. *Bless Me, Ultima.* Berkeley, CA: Tonatiuh-Quinto Sol International Publishers.

——— 1977. The Writer's Landscape: Epiphany in Landscape. *Latin American Literary Review* 5 (10):98–102.

Basso, Keith. 1976. "Stalking with Stories": Names, Places and Moral Narratives among the Western Apache. *Text, Play, and Story: The Construction and Reconstruction of Self Society*, ed., E. Bruner, 19–55. Washington, D.C.: The American Ethnological Society.

———1988. "Speaking with Names": Language and Landscape among the Western Apache. *Cultural Anthropology* 3 (2):99–130.

Berndt, R. 1976 Territoriality and the Problem of Demarcating Sociocultural Space. *Tribes and Boundaries in Australia*, ed., N. Peterson, 133–161. Atlantic Highlands: Humanities Press, Inc.

Deloria, Vine, Jr. 1975. *God is Red.* New York: Dell Publishing Company.

Feld, Steve. 1982. *Sound and Sentiment: Weeping, Poetics, and Song in Kaluli Expression.* Philadelphia: University of Pennsylvania Press.

Kluckhohn, Clyde and Dorothea Leighton. 1962. [revised edition of 1946]. *The Navaho.* New York: Doubleday and Company, Inc.

McLendon, Sally. 1977. Cultural Presuppositions and Discourse Analysis: Patterns of Presupposition and Assertion of Information in Eastern Pomo and Russian Narrative. *Linguistics and Anthropology*, ed., M. Saville-Troike, 153–89. Washington, D.C.: Georgetown University Press.

Momaday, N. Scott. 1976. Native American Attitudes to the Environment. *Seeing with a Native Eye: Essays on Native American Religion*, ed., W. H. Capps, 79–85. New York: Harper and Row, Publishers.

Munn, Nancy. 1973. *Walbiri Iconography: Graphic Representation and Cultural Symbolism in a Central Australian Society.* Ithaca: Cornell University Press.

Ortiz, Alfonso. 1969. *The Tewa World: Space, Time Being, and Becoming in Pueblo Society.* Chicago: The University of Chicago Press.

Ortiz, Simon. 1978. *Howbah Indians.* Tucson: Blue Moon Press, Inc.

Schiefflin, Edward. 1979. Mediators as Metaphors: Moving a Man to Tears in Papua, New Guinea. *The Imagination of Reality: Essays in Southeast Asian Coherence Systems*, eds., A. Becker and A. Yengoyan, 127–44. Norwood: Ablex Publishing Company.

Silko, Leslie M. 1986. Landscape, History and the Pueblo Imagination. In *Antaeus*, ed., D. Halpern, pp. 83–94. New York.

Smith, Patricia. 1988. "Commentary on 'Women's Place by Vera Norwood.'" In *Western Women: Their Land, Their Lives*, eds., L. Schlissel, J. Monk, and V. Ruiz, 189–95. Albuquerque: University of New Mexico Press.

Smith, Robert J. 1975. *The Art of the Festival.* University of Kansas Publications in Anthropology Number 6. Lawrence: University of Kansas Libraries.

Takaki, M. 1984. Regional Names in Kalinga: Certain Social Dimensions of Place-names. *Naming Systems*, ed., E. Tooker, 55–77. Washington, D.C.: American Ethnological Society.

Worth, Sol and John Adair. 1972. *Through Navajo Eyes: An Exploration in Film Communication and Anthropology*. Bloomington: Indiana University Press.

Young, M. Jane. 1985. Images of Power and the Power of Images: The Significance of Rock Art for Contemporary Zunis. *Journal of American Folklore* 98:3-48.

———1988. *Signs from the Ancestors: Zuni Cultural Symbolism and Contemporary Perceptions of Rock Art*. Albuquerque: University of New Mexico Press.

WORKS OF FICTION THAT DEAL WITH NATIVE-AMERICAN "PLACE"

Anaya, Rudolfo A. *Bless Me, Ultima*. Berkeley, CA: Tonatiuh-Quinto Sol International Publishers, 1972.

>This novel, which is somewhat autobiographical in parts, centers on the coming of age of a young Hispanic boy who lives in east-central New Mexico. Throughout the novel Anaya discusses the deep relationship human beings have with their particular places and landscapes—a relationship he describes in terms of kinship and the power of the earth, as reflected in the landscape, to transform people. For Anaya and his characters, the landscape is timeless and has the sort of "affecting presence" that remains always in their memory and opens their eyes to a special kind of vision and experience—an "epiphany."

Momaday, N. Scott. *The Names*. New York: Harper and Row, 1976.

>Described as a memoir of Momaday's life, this book is a beautiful portrayal of the names of significant people and places that shaped the author's life as he was growing up. Past and present are interwoven in an intense and moving portrait of the plains environment that was (and is) a place of magic and excitement for this man. Underlying this story of growing up is a deeper story that has to do with the Native American attitude to the land, to place, as forming the essential beauty and value of life.

——— *The Way to Rainy Mountain*. Albuquerque: University of New Mexico Press, 1969.

>This novel depicts a metaphysical journey across the plains undertaken by the Kiowa people. Intertwined with this metaphysical journey is the actual journey undertaken by these people as they were forced to give up their land and religion due to the actions of European-Americans. Here Momaday emphasizes that a peoples' relationship to the landscape—of which they are an integral part—informs who they are and who they dare to be. This poetically written book delineates significant landmarks—of the soul and

the physical journey that one makes—that tie the human spirit to a particular place and time—gone, in one sense, but forever enduring in another more mystical dimension.

Silko, Leslie Marmon. *Ceremony*. New York: Viking Press, 1977.

Although this novel focuses on the power of ceremonies and storytelling, it also highlights the importance of the pueblo as a homeplace. Silko poignantly discusses the problems caused for Native Americans who have been apart from that homeplace fighting in World War II—having been physically and spiritually torn from the pueblo, when they return from the war these veterans can no longer "fit" into the world they once had known. Particularly striking in this novel is Silko's equation of the place on the reservation where uranium mining has occurred with a grueseome ceremony of witchcraft enacted by those who no longer belong to this land.

Nomenclature

ERNEST SPECK

The procession of signs along our roads
Proclaiming the names of countless
Waterways, wet and dry,
Glorify a plethora of folk and things.

Mulligan's Draw and Skunk Hollow
Suggest that the polecat deserves
Memorializing as much as Mr. Mulligan.
But if Miller and Reed and all their tribes
Are long since dead and gone how can
Their creeks glorify them if we know
Not whom we glorify?
Do the progeny of Old Man Brown
Exult that their ancestor is acclaimed
In the somewhat obscene label Brown Hollow?
The origin of naming can be so vague
That Wright's Creek later became
Rice Creek, though far from the nearest paddy.
But worse, Six Mile Creek,
Seven miles beyond Three Mile Creek, and
Board Branch, named for a sawmill,
Suggest our desperate search for nomenclature.

But names are needed;
I'm glad I was born on
The banks of Dreary Hollow
And not on Stream #47623

Left to right: Two old "Quien Sabe" hands posing after a cow works near Garden City — Will Medlin, my uncle, and Zack Monroe — taken about 1909.

Fisher Pollard, noted bronc rider, at a rodeo in Juarez, Mexico in 1910.

John Patterson and Red Oak at Ranch on Centralia Draw, Stiles, Texas, 1943. Now at age 86, he is the oldest man around Big Lake still on his feet and at himself.

Sometimes I Get Lonesome For Lonesome

PAUL PATTERSON

*As if a man had fixed his face
In many a solitary place
Against the wind and open sky*

Maybe Wordsworth was searching for a sense of place when he wrote those words. Is there a system, a sensation, a sentiment, a method, a process by which, with which or in which one achieves, attains or arrives at a sense of place? Is it a matter of judgment, sentiment, hunch, horoscope? As for myself, a confirmed romanticist, all sentiment and no judgment, I played it by ear, "blown about by every wind of doctrine," so to speak, and relied on instinct, environment, heredity, climate, or any one or all of the five senses to arrive at a sense of my place. Eighty-four places I have called home in the course of eighty-plus years which averages out at about one and one-twentieth of a home per year. Can one exist in one-twentieth of a home? All things are possible to God; also to a family existing on an income not adequate for half as many. Yes, eighty-four homes of fifty-seven varieties ranging from the one-room, dirt-floor shanty in Stiles, Texas in 1911, to a country villa in Italy, owned by Count Ciano, son-in-law of Benito Mussolini in 1945, which increased my stature not one cubit though I did advance in rank from private to corporal. Of these eighty-four places, thirty-six were arrived at by covered wagon which also counted as a home and involved twenty-two towns and cities, nine ranches, six chuck wagons, three muleskinner camps, one sheepherder's tent, five bachelors' dives and two homes decent enough for a wife. There is more: ten military establishments, two liberty ships at sea and one great ocean liner, unescorted, freight train-temporary homes, eight boarding houses to "leaven the lump." Every single place had a common denominator—they were in lonesome country of some kind or for some reason.

My beginnings were truly a matter of lonesome country. My first sense of place—any place—was a potentially watery grave at the bottom of Kircheville Place tank in Reagan County in 1912 after I had attempted to walk on water. This attempt to emulate our Lord was not an act of faith nor an act of daring but an act of stupidity. The moss-covered surface I took to be solid ground. I had gone to the rescue of my favorite stick horse which my brother Fush had tossed into the water. Horses, even stick horses, were early a part of place for me. Our Rock Island brand wagon with its tattered canvas bonnet, washtub earrings and stovepipe necklace was met and/or passed on more West Texas roads than that of the crockery peddler. From Stiles proper, if you could call a dirt-floored cabin proper, to the Bates Place out of Big Lake to Salt Well below Rankin to the Powell place west of Rankin to the KCMO section house east of Rankin to the Doc Johnson Place south of Rankin, to Rankin proper, to the John R. Johnston place southeast of Upland to the Taylor place east of Upland to Upland proper—proper in every sense of the word—in downtown Upland in the bottom story of the jail with indoor bathroom facilities. My dad was deputy sheriff-bookkeeper-jailer.

I thought I had found my place in Upland proper, forever I hoped. By the time I started to school, Upland boasted a population of thirty, eight or ten of whom were of scholastic age. School attendance fluctuated between eight and ten students, the fluctuators being Bill and Pat Collins, sons of a homesteading widow possessed of a T Model Ford automobile, a rambling spirit and a roving eye. Midland was a great city of some seven hundred souls and was forty miles to the north with a railroad running straight over it and alongside the tracks stood stock pens with room enough to hold four thousand big steers—provided the train itself didn't booger them over it. Better yet, square in the middle of Midland stood what they called a confectionery where a body could—if he had five cents—buy himself what Bill and Pat called an ice cream comb. But forty miles away! As inaccessible as the moon now that Papa's wagon wanderlust had been arrested—at least for the moment. In the scheme of things, it was only a moment, but I was marked for lonesome forever. The place decreased in size over the years but the bigger it grew in my heart. Now it is almost a ghost town but still enfolded in the boundless bosom of cow country which is all that matters.

Things were even better, even more lonesome, when the family moved to Rankin, if you can believe it. Close to Rankin a prayer was answered; a long, longed-for dream come true. I got my first cowboy job at the age of seventeen with the Bar L. I was going to get to ride horses and ride them in lonesome places. The dream turned into a nightmare because of the horse-dream-come true. Thirty days later into the troubled mind and out between grim sun-blistered lips passed a stanza of my once-favorite song, "Sam Bass" who left Indiana to become a cowboy and then turned outlaw. "And I can damned well see why he turned outlaw"—this from the same grim lips, not to mention clenched teeth. Already throwed off four times and anybody who is any judge of horse conduct can see ol' Friday is fixin' to make it number five, thought I to myself; hence the song. A horse can tell by the smell. I had advice. "Paul, when a son of a bitch throws you off hold onto them reins spite'n hell. Git up, git back on and ride on. Never, never show back up in camp afoot. A disgrace." In flagrant violation of the code as cited by old Bill Wyatt, I got up and lunged at the beast, hoping to booger him off so I could walk the remaining seven miles home, in peace and safety. Adverse planetary aspects! All the imps of hell in connivance with the horse, saw to it that I remounted and rode the full distance at a snail's pace, needless to say, least I offend the beast. The last three miles were in plain sight to the boss's mother who waited dinner on me. In any case the first four falls, the latter fall and/or the delayed dinner prompted Lee to fire me. And promptly. My brother, John, wise in the ways of cowboys and horses said Lee hired me from the goodness of his heart, and fired me for the same reason—whatever that meant.

As with the other Paul, the Apostle, I had learned that whatsoever state that I was in, therewith to be content. Now I was content to a certain extent. I was content to get my high school diploma. Congenial companionship and activities to share it with in Rankin had made the life of this Paul a ball but had not completely silenced the clarion call to cowboy in lonesome country. And by graduation night my destiny was set in stone. 'Ere the echo of our commencement speaker's admonitions had died, our hero was high-tailing it for the old O'Brien homestead place at the foot of King Mountain, never more to look a schoolhouse in the door. This time not as a common cow plod but my own boss, master of all I surveyed, ninety-nine percent of which was done a horseback! However, nine days and nights without sight of human face, form or female figure brought shades of the Ancient Mariner at sea—"So lonely 't was that God Himself scarce seemed there to be." Frankly, it wasn't God's companionship I was missing, but beings in human form, specifically, female. Even lonesome country had a few women.

More horse falls, a couple of which were close calls, in fact too close to call, almost persuaded me that this might not be my calling after all. Then another close call forty miles out of Ozona proved the determining factor. Ozona, too, is known for lonesome. A big gray horse with an unprintable name and an A.C. Hoover brand jobbed my head in a rocky road bed. I came to, to a certain extent, with a burning yearning for learning, hence my matriculation from Sul Ross in 1931 only to learn that the cowboy flame flickered, faintly yet. Throughout that year the closest working touch I came to cow work were cows' teats at Burgess Dairy. At least I was keeping cowboy hours, and then some—2:30 to 8:30 A.M.—a pleasant eight-hour break for learning, not taking into account the four-mile stroll to and from. Then back to the back end of a cow from 4:30 to 9:30 P.M. followed by another couple of hours of sleeplessness worrying about that damned 2:30 A.M. glaring me in the face. Besides, cows weren't really my interest. Horses were. Any cowboy knows that. College graduation was a rare occasion indeed, even in good times much less way out in lonesome country during the Great Depression.

Now what? No work to be had in lonesome country either a horseback or afoot. No market for cattle, no market for sheep, except from the federal government, at seventeen dollars per cow and four dollars per sheep. Uncle Sam had no earthly use for that many livestock except to feed his nieces and nephews, one fourth of whom were jobless, with a great percentage of them hungry and living in lonesome country. Instead of feeding his children, Uncle Sam slaughtered and buried cows and sheep on the spot. This kill off program was not to appease the appetites of the hungry but to stimulate the economy and create jobs. What it did was create a controversy that is argued over to this day. There was no market for horses either but theirs was a similar fate; driven off to cheaper grass supposedly which really meant driven off to die of slow starvation.

No market for livestock, no horses to break or break me, no cows to punch, no sheep to herd, so I would teach school. The school, the Blackwell school which was strictly Hispanic and segregated, was in lonesome Marfa, Texas. The area was encompassed round about by cow country, exclusively, and the finest in Texas. Lest I go loco from lonesome, I had but to walk out to the edge of town, soak up sight, smells and sounds and glory in the silence.

I was taken right in the community, what there was of it, at Granny Humphrey's Boarding House. They took me in and then took me right down to rodeo headquarters and got me signed on to ride a bull. Those folks were sure good to a stranger.

Next stop was Sanderson where I moved up to principal of another segregated Hispanic elementary school. I was not entirely new to Sanderson. I had once chosen it as a Christmas vacation spot over Fort Davis which was more lonesome. A feller needs to get into a crowd once in a while especially at Christmas. There was much to be admired in Sanderson—rugged ranch country heritage, fighting frontier background, south-of-the-border charm, hospitable hosts, good children to teach. Who could ask for anything more? Nobody. But something more arrived on an October night. It was the sweetest music this side of Guy Lombardo's Royal Canadians—Southern Pacific freight train music. Nightly, locomotive whistle music; music so enchanting that Sanderson's encircling mountains fashioned each note into six, sometimes eight encores. Sometimes I stayed awake purposely to savor the Southern Pacific freight's siren sound played across lonesome country. Then, come spring, three of us succumbed.

Bright and early one May morning my compañeros and I "nailed a drag" north, to lead the jolly, carefree life of a hobo. Destination Detroit. One was going to buy a new auto, one went along for the ride. As for myself, I was launching a new career, hoboing, something no man could possibly fail at. But I could and did. I found no sense of place any place on any rail we rode. Nor did I find comfort and convenience in any of their accommodations—gondolas, reefers, side door pullmans, cattle cars. Nor did I receive any accommodation from their employees, chief amongst whom were the railroad bulls. But at least I was receptive to suggestion. When a bull on two occasions pointed a pistol at us then at the highway and barked "hit and git," I hit it and got. I could take a hint.

On the positive side, this trip sharpened my sense of place for Sanderson even more. It was to be the place where I would woo, win and would have wed on the spot one, Marjorie Mixon, commercial teacher. But in Sanderson it was not unlawful to wed, but to teach in a wedded condition with the one wedded to. So, I sallied forth to the Booger Y to summer roundup hoping to kill two birds with one stone. Number one, to enjoy being back in the saddle again and number two, to somehow insinuate myself and bride into the Crane school system. I got a job and for me it was this hero's seventh heaven—lonesome in a sandhills setting. For my bride, the location was shaky since she was a deep East Texas piney woods girl who cried for two days straight upon being introduced to my paradise—West Texas. Some people fear heights; some people fear depths. She feared widths such as thirty miles between towns and even farther between trees.

There were other places, lots of them, and other kinds of living to be done even in other countries. There was peace and war, but always a return to lonesome country. After all these years and eighty-four moves, the place that holds first place is the old O'Brien homestead and the bachelor's dive where I was master of my fate and boss of all I surveyed—twenty-three saddle horses and 304 head of cattle. What is more I was sole initiator of all the action be it a horseback or afoot, preferably the former. However, from the perspective of maturity it was not the action packed days that stir fond recollections. It was the tranquil nights while I was stretched upon my soogans savoring of the serenity, the solitude, the silence, and whatsoever sound stemmed therefrom in West Texas cow country of space, good horses to ride, cattle to know. In recollection, it is the sounds of breaking silence, the dead of night silence, by such creatures as Biggun, bull of the greasewoods, king of King Mountain, bogeyin' in to water.

"Ooahooahooahooahooahooahooahooahooahooah"—rumbling in his throat like time, seemed to have no beginning and no end. A constant low-thunder sound like the purring of a 2000 pound tomcat. But unlike my two tomkitten bunk mates, Biggun's purring was not from contentment. Biggun was on the prod, though God only knows why. Nothing on this wide earth to do but eat and make love with his choice of 260 sweethearts all within beck and call. His fourteen rivals may as well have been cows as far as horning in on his honeymoons were concerned. Every once in a while mind's eye and natural ear would catch the big picture, so to speak. Biggun's nose pointed up and mouth trailing silver slobbers, he would let go with three, sometimes four, high-pitched "eeah, eeah, eeahs." I have yet to fathom his message. Accompaniment to Biggun's arias varied. One time it might be a coyote duet or a dozenette. Impossible for human ear to determine. Again it might be the lonesome night horse pleading for companionship. Or it could be an owl, or the windmill groaning against its water load. The crickets were so constant in their song that it seemed part of the silence.

I am marked, just like a brand, by this country, these sights and sounds. Sometimes I get lonesome for lonesome, just like Wordsworth, and fix my face "in many a solitary place against the wind and open sky."

To An Old Friend

RED STEAGALL

I stood by the fountain as they brought him in,
A lost lonely look on his face.
I ain't never seen him in nothin' but boots.
The wheelchair shore seemed out of place.

It took him awhile to recall who I am,
But confusion turned into a grin.
It was tho we were saddled up, ready to ride,
The Hackberry Pasture again.

He laughed as he said, "I remember the time
That yeller bronc swallered his head,
And pitched you so high that you turned over twice.
Me'n Benny Bob swore you was dead."

He looked up at me and asked, "How is old Ben?"
I lied and said, "He's doin' fine."
No need to remind him his brother was gone.
Ben died back in seventy nine.

For most of an hour we rode at a trot.
We branded and shaped up the steers,
Drank gallons of coffee, ate sourdough bread,
And cowboyed for 51 years.

I thot he's an old man when I was a kid,
At a time when I needed a friend.
He took me to raise, taught me all that I know,
'bout horses and cattle and men.

My daddy had died and I needed a job.
I'se big for a kid of fifteen.
They put me to work on the four 6's Ranch—
Was dumb as a gourd and as green.

We's lookin' for strays in the Wichita Breaks—
Was me and John Gaither and him.
I lost sight of John so I'se lookin' around
'A daydreamin; there on the rim.

Rode up on some cattle hid out in the brush—
A two year old steer come by me.
Throwed a nine in his tail and cut a new trail,
Right out through the salt cedar trees.

I took in behind him a givin' it hell—
The colt I was ridin' was green.
I thot to myself, he ain't getting away—
This roan is a running machine.

Was goin' full bore when we got to the bank—
The stream wasn't wide as my hat.
I nearly pulled up, but I thot, What the Hell,
I've jumped rivers wider than that.

I bogged that old pony plumb up to his gut—
Was wallerin' and thrashin' around.
He's goin' down deeper with each desperate lunge,
Me prayin' he'd find solid ground.

Just at the moment that I heard his voice,
A rope appeared right by the roan.
"Get outa that kack and hang on to my line.
The colt'll get out on his own."

I've crossed that old river a many a time.
I've found me a bog once or twice.
But I still remember that thirty foot rope
And this cowboy piece of advice:

"When you ride the river, son, make sure your horse
Is gentle and seasoned as well,
'Cause only the good ones will get you across.
That quicksand goes clean down to hell."

I got up to leave and he reached for my hand.
Said, "Son, I'm sure glad you dropped by.
If you see old Ben, have him saddle my horse,
I hate sittin' waitin' to die."

His voice started crackin, he swallered and said,
"I'm nearin' the end of my ride.
If I cross the river before you get there,
I'll leave a good horse on this side."

The Memories in Grandmother's Trunk

RED STEAGALL

They came in a wagon from St. Jo, Missouri
Grandmother was seven years old.
I remember she said she walked most of the way
Through the rain, and the mud and the cold.

She saw the Comanche, they came into camp—
Not the savage she'd seen in her dreams.
They were ragged and pitiful, hungry and cold,
Begging for salt pork and beans.

They staked out a claim at the cross timbers breaks
Where the big herds went north to the rail.
One day a cowpuncher gave her a calf
Too young to survive on the trail.

Their Jersey cow gave more milk than they needed—
The calf grew up healthy and strong.
She staked him that fall in the grass by the creek
And pampered him all winter long.

In April her daddy rode into Fort Worth
With her calf on the end of his rope.
He traded her prize for a red cedar trunk
That she filled full of memories and hope.

I found grandmother's trunk hidden under a bed
In a back room where she used to sleep.
I've spent the whole morning reliving her youth
Through the trinkets that she fought to keep.

There's the old family bible, yellowed and worn,
On the first page was her family tree.
She'd traced it clear back to the New England coast
And the last entry she made was me.

I unfolded a beautiful star pattern quilt—
In the corner she cross stitched her name.
I wonder how many children it kept safe and warm
From the cold of the west Texas plain.

There's a tattered old picture that says "Mom, I Love You."
Tho' faded, there's a young soldier's face,
And a medal of honor the government sent
When he died in a faraway place.

A cradle board covered with porcupine quills,
Traded for salt pork and beans,
Was laying on top of a ribbon that read,
Foard County Rodeo Queen.

Dried flowers pressed in a book full of poems,
A card with this message engraved,
To my darlin' wife on our 25th year,
And some old stamps my grandfather saved.

Of course there are pictures of her daddy's folks.
They sure did look proper and prim.
I reckon if they were to come back to life
We'd look just as funny to them.

Grandmother's life seemed so simple and slow
But the world started changin' too soon.
She heard the first radio, saw the first car
And lived to see men on the moon.

Life on this planet is still marching on,
And I hope that my grandchildren see
My side of life through the trinkets I've saved
The way grandmother's trunk does for me.

New York, New York

CLAY REYNOLDS

Excerpted from the novel Texas Augustus

*M*y birthday is August first, and I was half past forty-two when I realized that Pease City had disappeared. It was a disquieting discovery, starting out as vaguely unsettling and then exploding into a kind of panic that tended to burn from somewhere near my stomach with a raging fury. It was as if part of me had disappeared as well, slipped away forever, and it took me maybe a half an hour to quiet down and think the whole problem through.

I hadn't been back to Texas for eight years, if you don't count layovers in Houston International or DFW. The closest I had been to the land where I was born and raised—or, properly, reared—was when I saw a couple of films Horton Foote wrote a few years back. They were shot down in Waxahachie, south of Dallas, and in spite of the fact that the location was a full three hundred miles from Pease City, the land bore certain similarities to my childhood recollections, enough at least to make me misty-eyed and nostalgic over a beer at Sardi's afterwards. I almost never drink beer in New York. That's how soft and squishy I was feeling inside. I sort of felt I needed something from home to hang onto. I tried to get my friends, who had come into the city with us just to see the movie to go down on Fifth Avenue South to the Lone Star Cafe with me, but they said it was too late to go that far downtown, and they were right. I settled for lecturing the Sardi's bartender on the exquisite taste of Lone Star beer while I sipped a Budweiser and dreamed of home while my friends talked about acting techniques in neo-westerns. I felt sad.

But I didn't think much about home even then. I mean, I always meant to get back to Pease City one day or another, but there were so many places, here and abroad, I also wanted to see, and I couldn't afford the time just to go out among the mesquite and prickly pear of north central Texas. My parents had died years ago, and my only relative remaining in Sandhill County was a second cousin named Klute, and to tell the truth, I never was sure whether Klute was his first or last name.

On the wall of my office which is on the fourteenth floor in midtown, over on Lexington Avenue, I kept a big *National Geographic* map of the United States. In bright red marker, I had traced every trip I had ever taken by car or bus anywhere in the continental U.S., Mexico, or Canada. Parts of the country, especially the eastern seaboard, were criss-crossed with red markings, so thick in some places that town names and highway numbers were no longer legible. New England was like that, and so was Virginia and the "border" states of Kentucky and Tennessee. So also was Texas. I had at some point in my forty-two years driven every major highway in the state, from Boca Chica to Texline, from Orange to El Paso, from Texarkana to the Big Bend Country. I had been in Amarillo, Victoria, Houston, Odessa, Longview, Plainview, Prairie View, Lubbock, San Antonio, Harlingen, Fort Stockton, and Wichita Falls—God Knows I'd been to Wichita Falls. No one ever forgets being in Wichita Falls, but all of that was long before I was married, before I moved to New York.

I'd also been in Cut 'N Shoot, Earth, and Dime Box, Seminole, Big Springs, Roaring Springs, Sweetwater, Sour Lake, and Mineral Wells. I'd at least driven through Comanche, Paducah, Nocona, Quanah, Geronimo, and Shawnee Prairie. I'd also been in Paris, Rome, and Italy, both Texas cities by those names and the European prototypes, and I'd had lunch in Windthorst, slept in motels in Whitesboro, Jacksboro, and Hillsboro, and once I fixed a flat in Cool, Texas when the thermometer was topping 103. I had crossed the Brazos, Guadalupe, Rio Grande, Red, Sabine, Neches, Trinity, San Antonio, and Nueces Rivers more times than I could count, and I had been swimming or boating on a healthy number of the lakes. After all, I was a Texan by birth and residence for almost twenty-five of my years at least, and I felt I was part of it. But seeing Pease City disappear from the map when I unfolded my new *Travel Club Roadguide* and began planning our annual trip to Maine (I instinctively glance down at Texas just to make sure it's still as big as I remembered it), I was shocked beyond words to see the city gone.

My first reaction, after the panic subsided, was to confirm the *Roadguide*'s error. I buzzed Marge and sent her out to find as many maps of Texas and the Southwest as she could locate, and I then called five or six travel clubs listed in the yellow pages. I made the hapless girls on the other end of the phone line search their own atlases and road maps, but on none of them did poor little Pease City remain. It was gone. Blipped off the red and blue and green traces of cartography programs on travel club computers. I expressed outrage to each club I called, but their sympathies were hardly a match for the depression I was feeling.

When Marge got back with a dozen different maps, I scanned each one and flung it across the room in anger. Pease City was just gone. I went over to my wall map and squinted at the black dot that indicated where it had been with its name neatly printed in minuscule type across what I knew but the map-maker did not know was Blind Man's Creek. It was still there on my wall at least. The *National Geographic* hadn't let me or my hometown down. Or had they? This map was almost ten years old and had replaced another one only because my original plan to stick pins in cities I had visited had finally destroyed the first map. I called the National Geographic Society, and they checked, and they confirmed my worst fears. Pease City no longer existed, at least it no longer existed so long as map-makers were concerned.

"How large a place is it?" the girl at the Society asked me.

"Oh, not too big," I replied casually but seriously, "It never was too big, but it's always been there. It was a B high school."

I could have kicked myself for adding that. This chick had a British accent and probably thought a football was round. Besides, the high school had closed two years after I graduated, and all the kids went into Agatite, for their last four years, anyway.

"Let me check the census report." I heard the click of computer keys.

"This doesn't show that anyone lives there," she said with a false ring of concern in her voice. "Are you sure we're spelling it correctly?"

"In the old days, it was spelled Pease City," I said. "I don't think it's changed."

She checked and clicked again.

"Nope," she said. "It's not here. How long has it been since you were there?"

"Eight or ten," I fudged. "Look, I've got one of your old maps on my office, and it's right there where it ought to be. It's right between the Pease and the Red rivers, just off the Cap Rock."

"Just off the what?"

"Cap Rock, Great Plains, Llano Estacado, Indian Country! Goddamnit is there anybody there who knows anything about geography? You are the National *Geographic* Society, for Chrissake."

"There is no reason to swear at me, sir." Her voice was as cool and sour as a fresh grapefruit.

"I'm sorry. Look, is there anyone there who can tell me who made the decision to drop this little town off your new maps?"

She paused for a moment. "I can let you talk to Dr. Fielding, but he's only in charge of the publication of the maps. I'm not sure who makes them up."

"Fine," I said, "Put me through to him."

She did, but naturally he was in a meeting. At any given time in New York City, half the working people are in a meeting with the other half. The same is true in California, I've learned, and I made a mental note to tell Marge that she was never to say to anyone who called me that I was "in a meeting," even if I was.

His secretary was marginally more helpful and marginally less British than the first girl I talked to. At least she explained that when the census of a town fell below one hundred, they generally dropped it from the map, unless, of course, it had historical significance. Did Pease City have any such significance? I searched my mind, but except for one time when a cattleman named McAllen shot down a cattle rustler in the main street—and that was sometime around the turn of the century—I couldn't think of a historical event that had any significance.

She was patient enough, but she still wouldn't let me talk to Fielding, and only promised to give him my message, and that was that. As far as the National Geographic Society was concerned, Pease City had ceased to exist.

I paced back and forth and then went over and pushed up my office window. It was late December, and it was cold. Snow, wet and thick, swirled down through the Manhattan streets, but it never reached the black bundles that scurried up and down the concrete sidewalks below. "This ain't snow," Perry Clark, my friend from Maine, had chided me when I first came to New York and commented on the fat wet flakes as they blew past my window. "This is shit. It's shittin' on you. White shit." A quick walk over to the Stage Deli at lunch confirmed what he said. It wasn't even that cold, just wet. The snow kept a respectable distance some ten or fifteen stories off the street, and the New Yorkers hated it. One thing I learned quickly about New Yorkers: They have no capacity for dealing with the weather. As a Texan, I was born with it.

My window was one of my favorite things. In the summer, when the temperature soared to a stifling ninety-degrees, I was fond of throwing it open and propping up a circulation fan on the sill. It drove my colleagues wild, and Marge refused to come into the office at all. The building super made me stop that. He said it was too hard on the air conditioning. He didn't say much in the spring or the fall, since they shut the a/c off anyway—or so I suspected—and in the winter not even a hardy Texan is stupid enough to sit around and let the New York wind inside. But I still liked to open it up from time to time, especially when it's snowing—or "shitting"—and watch the white wetness fall and melt in what too damned many people have called the Concrete Canyons of Manhattan. "It pleasures me" or so my grandmother used to say.

It's a temporary pleasure at best, though. For this building, we've been told, is scheduled to be imploded or something that will reduce it to rubble within the next year or so. The owners are desperately afraid that somebody is going to get wise to the fact that it's over eighty years old and try to put it in the National Historical Register or something. That would keep them from tearing it down and building one of those glass and steel things on the same property, something that will quadruple their rents and increase their tax write-offs at the same time. In the new building where I'll either move or move back into, the windows won't open at all, at least not on purpose.

As I looked out into the snowy atmosphere, I recalled that the windows in my mother's house in Pease City wouldn't open either. She had them painted shut back during the depression when the dust storms would come roaring in over the prairie like great black clouds. I'd like to see New Yorker's deal with one of those mothers. After the dust settled into conservation-wise fields and air conditioning was invented, she kept them sealed—even in her "new" house in Agatite where we moved her, but now she wanted to keep the cold air in, and nothing I or my sister could say would persuade her to open them. We were scared to death the house would catch fire and she couldn't get out, but by the time we were old enough to worry about it, she was too frail and sick to open a sash window anyway, so we just let it go.

I tried to lean way out the window and smell some fresh air. But the air was cold and damp and didn't really have much odor, at least none I could recognize. It just smelled like New York. Every big city has its own particular odor, I've discovered. Chicago smells different from Boston which smells different from Philadelphia which smells different from Washington, D.C., which smells different from Atlanta, which smells different from L.A. And so forth. But New York's smell was different. It was dirty—that it shared with most of the other cities—but there were other smells also. Hot dogs from street venders, and chestnuts, and pretzels, and bagels, and Italian restaurants, and Chinese, and Jewish delis, and all of it. From time to time the smell of the Hudson or East River would come wafting down 49th Street, and that could make me gag. But it was a New York smell, all right. I had noticed it the first day I came to the city, and I had gotten used to it. I suddenly felt damp and cold inside as well, I'd been in New York too long. To my horror, I realized that I couldn't remember what Texas smelled like.

NEIGHBORHOOD

Neighborhood ... a smaller territory snipped out of the larger fabric of place. **Neil Daniel** *tells of neighborhoods and defines perimeters bounded by sidewalks and fences.* **Betsy Colquitt** *considers poetically the cultural and age perspectives of neighborhoods in a city.* **Duane Bidwell** *who has written for a city newspaper, speaks for a man who finds his sense of place in a community. The story would be in no way unusual if Tawee were not a Buddhist monk in a monastery in a relocated Laotian village on the prairies of North Texas. In poetry,* **Jan Seale** *identifies a couple whose neighborhood covers acres, rows and miles, and each other.* **Joyce Roach,** *in a short story, tells of the Promised Land where a child is protected from the horrors of war, where all are healed by the laying on of rural hands.*

Neighborhood

NEIL DANIEL

*P*art of what shapes my life is geography. I live in Ryan Place, an urban neighborhood close to the center of Fort Worth. A middle-sized neighborhood in a Midwestern city where middle-class values cling like the roots of grass or ivy to the concrete and bricks that pave our parking spaces. This city neighborhood was shaped by the era in which it was born. The streets form a grid of long narrow blocks that made it easy to walk to the streetcar lines. The houses are lined up an even distance from the street on narrow lots. Sidewalks parallel the streets as far as you can see, sidewalks that once carried most of the traffic before every family had two or more cars. Between the sidewalk and the curb are trees of various ages—elms, hackberries, an occasional oak—planted at odd times during the last fifty years. Some of the trees are young and ambitious, second or third generation trees, stabbing roots down beneath the street, raising strong limbs to join a canopy that arches over Fifth Avenue, nearly unbroken for most of a mile. Many of the old trees display the wear of age and violent weather, circular scars, like portholes, where lower limbs were cut off because they interfered with traffic, long gashes where limbs have been torn off by high winds.

The geography of my life is a mix of social forces and outdoor nature.

The people of Ryan Place live a good deal in their yards. Because the houses are close together, the lots narrow, we don't have spacious lawns. No one in the neighborhood owns a tractor mower; there is no room to maneuver such a machine. Each lot backs up to an alley, where the city used to pick up the trash. The utility companies still use the alleys to maintain telephone lines and read gas meters. Mainly the alleys are preserve for wild life: neighborhood cats, rats and mice to be sure, and a dense population of squirrels. And children who appreciate the overgrown tunnel created by the trees and bushes that line the alleys.

The people also live a good deal on the streets. We have no lake, and we are some distance from the city parks. People in this neighborhood have gone out of their way to get to know their neighbors. When school is not in session, the kids are up and down the streets on bicycles, on skateboards, or on foot. Their parents know one another, and they visit from house to house, carrying a can of beer or the evening paper, sharing coffee in the mornings, offering advice about how to fix the car or replace a fuse in the dishwasher. Conscious of the precarious destiny of an older neighborhood, which developed between 1910 and World War I, the people in this part of the city have banded together to present a common front against the forces of urban erosion.

Over The Fence

Over the fence in the back yard I hear Kelly (7) and Erin (5) playing on their swing set and singing Stephen's Foster's "Swanee River." I haven't heard the song in years, almost since my own childhood. The children's singing lends me comfort and continuity. No matter what the pace of modern life, no matter how things change, some elements of a common culture link my childhood and theirs.

Erin insists that Marcella and I are her other grandparents. The song confirms her belief.

I have been thinking about roots as a way of getting into an essay on neighborhoods. We can work ourselves back to our beginnings in several ways.

We can finger through our family histories, making ethnic links, tracing kinship up and down and across the lattice of family relations. Like Alex Haley, we can follow our parents and their parents back to foreign homelands. My family pilgrimage would take me to Ireland, I think, and to Wales. I have made no effort to trace beyond two generations.

We can journey to the geographic sources of our own lives as well, returning to where we grew up or where our parents once lived. Lately I have traveled to a suburban neighborhood in Minneapolis and found still there the lakes and parks where I played as a boy nearly fifty years ago. With only a slight heaving of the imagination, I can visit Cincinnati, where my mother's family lived, and reconstruct the stories she told me about her turn-of-the-century childhood.

The third way we can return to our roots is by locating and entering the culture that gave us our beginning values. I am a lifetime resident of the neighborhood where I live even though I have been here only ten or fifteen years. A middle-class child of suburban professional parents and grandparents, now myself parent and grandparent of youngsters headed for middle-class life, I am both product and agent of life-ways that endure tenaciously in a section of the city that is neither inner city nor rambling suburb. The first time I came here, as an adult looking for a house, I stepped through time into the place of my childhood. I had been away for long decades, sampling the world, getting an education, trying out new personas. I came home to a place I had never been and discovered nothing had changed.

In this city pocket, neighbors play a dominant role. The culture thrives on covered-dish suppers and swapping baby-sitting duties and looking after each other's houses while the neighbors are away. The street I have lived on most of my life is devoted to well-kept lawns and freshly painted trim, though the sidewalks buckle and deteriorate. We meet on the streets to shake our fists at the teenagers who drive too fast. We grumble about the powers at city hall that continue to ignore our pleas for new curbs and pavement. We talk about the schools but try to avoid sex, religion, and national politics. We mention the weather several times a day.

I prefer not to be ethnocentric or exclusive in my observation. I don't suggest that my mediurban background represents all of America. This country is as much the blistering streets of South Side Chicago or of upper Manhattan as it is the shady lawns of Ryan Place in Fort Worth or Linden Hills in Minneapolis. Home for many Americans is the farmland around Plainview, Texas, or Findlay, Ohio. The neighborhood can be glossy San Francisco or Hispanic San Antonio or Beall Street in Memphis.

But I can't deny my roots, and I am learning not to be ashamed of them. For me home is a neighborhood close to the city, where a five-year-old and a seven-year-old pick the blossoms off our garden flowers, leaving the stems behind, and bring them to their honorary grandparents. Where a group of kids in camouflage fatigues guard a fort erected in a backyard tree. Where spring is announced by a flourish of lawnmowers and a congress of backyard cooks.

Home is where Kelly and Erin sing "Swanee River" on the swingset next door and pull on emotional strings buried deep in my heart.

Sidewalks

Russell Clark learned to ride a bicycle on the sidewalk of Fifth Avenue. A talented, well-balanced kid with a great sense of adventure, Russell would get on the sidewalk bike in front of his house, pointed northward, downhill, toward Cantey.

It was not a grown-up bicycle with a coaster brake, but a child's direct-drive model with the sprocket linked by chain to the back wheel. As the bike moved forward, the pedals would spin around. The only way to brake the speed was to pedal slower, resisting the forward momentum of the machine.

Russell gets on the bike in front of his house. His hands rest easily on the handlebars, his feet are out on both sides to balance. He walks the bike forward, pushing on the ground. When he gets up enough speed to balance, he raises his feet to place them on the pedals. It is not easy. The pedals are spinning as the bike moves, slapping repeatedly the bottoms of his feet. Meanwhile the bike is slowing slightly, weaving from side to side. Russell has his attention riveted on the sidewalk ahead, hoping he will not pitch onto the lawn in front of Mr. Blank's house or veer off into the street. Moving the handlebars from side to side for balance, he doesn't have much control over where he is going. And when he finally crash lands on the Ternamians' lawn he has to pick up his bike and walk it back home, uphill, so that he can start over.

He has bumped and rocked down the sidewalk, riding on solid rubber tires, uncushioned, taking a spanking because the sidewalk is in poor repair and the huge squares of concrete are tilted on the shifting earth.

Our sidewalks are training ground for other athletes as well. Sarah Longsworth was a terrific sidewalk roller skater in her younger days (she is a teen ager now and doesn't skate as often as she used to). She would labor up the hill toward Lowden, swinging her arms, pushing hard to make the hill. At the corner she would turn around and head back home, mostly coasting, shifting from one foot to the other as she crossed the cracks in the sidewalk where the squares do not meet evenly. She had to be agile and know the course to avoid being pitched forward on tender knees.

We are lucky to have sidewalks at all, of course. Our sidewalks are an attractive feature of Ryan Place. They connect us with the past, with a way of life preserved only in older neighborhoods. It is easier, somehow, to wander down the block, to visit with the Losoyas, to chat with ninety-year-old Mrs. Miller, because we don't have to do it in the street. Our sidewalk is a vital link.

Transcendence

Those familiar with educational philosophy know that Abraham Maslow's hierarchy of human needs includes, at the top, the need for transcendence, a concept easy to comprehend, difficult to define.

Central to transcendence is the awareness of order, wholeness, and something beyond the self. In a religious context it is what we call holiness; it makes us conscious of the presence of god. But you don't have to believe in God to experience transcendence. The consciousness that somehow the world goes together, that everything fits, is also transcendence.

Yesterday as I was walking with the dog, I encountered an ordinary suburban scene, a view down a street in Ryan Place, that made me aware of transcendence. Each house was unique, detached, but all were linked in a pattern—all about the same distance from the street, each with a well kept lawn, the lawns making a continuous green space punctuated by an occasional hedge or a bed of flowers. While we most likely associate transcendence with wilderness, with natural beauty rather than with civilized scenes, it is possible to perceive order, a sense of rightness, in city views. Humankind is a part of nature; that goes without saying. But the transcendent experience goes beyond that observation. Humans are rational and capable of artistic arrangement. But I think transcendent experience acknowledges an order beyond our conscious design. Just as in nature the wonder derives from our sudden apprehension of how things are, independent of any staged effects (no artist designs a mountain), so in the city we can catch glimpses of pattern and purpose that go beyond the planning of any single builder, architect, or homeowner; it is the cumulative affect of many individual and social forces.

Rows of houses or buildings set up patterns of replication even though each one is different and no one arranged them that way. Series repetitions of poles, signs, box cars; skylines of cities, silhouettes of heavy building equipment—earth movers on highways, giant cranes atop new buildings—no one plans such sights; they just happen. They happen, perhaps, mainly in the consciousness of the observer. They trigger the experience of transcendence.

Lewis Thomas touches on this phenomenon in his essays, particularly in "The Lives of a Cell." He equates the unconscious but apparently purposeful growth and development of human systems with the aggregate behavior of colonies of ants or bees. There is a harmony, a purpose, a curious rightness and integrity to the total (transcendent) activity of independent but related parts.

Everyone needs to experience transcendence. In particular, people deprived of the block-buster Hollywood effects of the sublime in nature need to be reminded that transcendence is available in any environment on any scale. It exists abundantly in our backyards.

Inner-City Scene: Fort Worth

BETSY COLQUITT

1. The Old Woman

In her present, little happens,
but past is an open book.
she reads its pages again

and again. No page records
last night's attack, and cheerful,
she turns today to long-ago page

about a marriage where she finds
her husband's praise for her many gifts
and his good counsel in whatever it was

she thinks she once did, could now
should she choose. Most worn page
holds children playing in its lines.

Harmony rules her nursery
where change never intrudes,
no hurt injures, absence is fantasy.

These remarkable, loving children
aging half a continent away
rarely leave this page, but if away,

telephone every Sunday.
Dead receiver links distant voices
to her distant present, brings

more than enough news for this week's
porch-sitting. Like the frontpage,
her news alters little day to day,
but names she invokes never change.

2. *Yard*

Next door, the couple who never much liked
one another don't now. Evenings their voices

quarrel like jays. Mornings they take silent turns
sweeping walks, the garden, anything

to escape the crowded house. Two people fill,
overfill it, and take it—whatever 'it' is—

out on the grass. Once 'it' was children,
a son, two daughters, their wings

clipped short to keep them aground.
But feathers grew back, and children fled.

Now no powermower cuts short enough to stop
the daily mowings, the grass crew-cut,

weeds scalped to roots by these rites,
mowers noisily fuming the neighborhood

with their furious flailing and cutting,
familiars for year.

3. The Black Family

Whatever else they're lively,
these adults, children all kin
though blood lines are obscure.

One motherly sort tries a few flowers,
but her plants encounter war—
oil cans, grease buckets, beer bottles,

remains of Kentucky Fried tossed
to seed in once-flowerbeds and grass.
Decibels ring dizzily in this yard,

house where loudest radios never
conquer the many voices, countless barks
of dogs hungry, fecund, unlicensed.

And there are cars, dismantled, always
in repair, their private parts
a Stonehenge boldly spread on a city lot.

Sometimes a car is put together,
speeds away, returns with others
to home there today. Meanwhile

garbage grows wings, a radiator patinas,
puppies and babies open shut eyes
to all wonders about them,

energy breeding, life living itself
as perpetually lively, lucky
in bringing forth the rarest blooms,

a daisy, some stock, defiant lantanas
that never learned they were not meant
to grow in this hard ground.

4. Guanajuato

Only the Tovar children are citizens,
could vote were they the age.
Their parents, their most extended family

transplanted here from Guanajuato
('where the mummies are') work, make do,
pay taxes, carry their green cards,

or lacking these, get taken back,
spend a night or two in Nuevo Laredo
and then return to this alien place

curiously turning into home. They'd
expected only money. These transplants
plant. Their flowers, children flourish.

Althea bushes, beds of vinca,
tall gladiolas parade on this homestead.
Even the youngest Tovar knows two names

for each flower, translates when needed.
It often is. But the parents dig in,
don't give up, are catching on to a tongue

they'll never learn to think in.
When the old woman next door
tells her latest news,

the parents listen, understand,
know there's no need to know her words.
The children know her vocabulary,

but her grammar of age is alien
to citizens rightfully claiming
the promise of their young world.

5. Nights

Nights are loud in her wreck
of a house. Old trees scour
the siding, scrape last paint away.
A screen springs loose,
a window raises,
and there's another sound
that never stops.

She hears it every night,
calm or windy, and listening
for it, sleeps restlessly.
But she doesn't scare.
Mornings she tells how her heart
acted up, the ambulance came,
and a hand fed her oxygen.

But this night, this hard hand
holds air away somewhere
in a faraway place she strains for,
can't quite reach,
and silence deafens.

Bedclothes tumble, and her gown.
She wants to say "I don't wash much,"
but speech holes up, hides
under this weight, this smell
that makes her feel bridal,

all her connections tearing
as wires, clothes, touch jumble
when this instrument probes secret parts.

Next morning on her porch
she tells of the night long ago
when coming home early, he surprised her.
But she knows she's more to tell
today of this story if her fingers
could turn the right page.

The Tovar children hear, school
in boredom, see new bruises, scratches
as like ones she shows everyday.
They know all her stories by heart,
can't wait to escape, to play.

Where the Buddha Dwells

DUANE BIDWELL

From where we sit on Tawee's porch, sucking sugarcane juice through straws, the North Texas prairie rolls and dips toward the horizon. Tawee's heavy robe is inside. He relaxes in the thin cotton jersey monks wear at all times. I undo a button of my Oxford shirt and push up the sleeves. We are quiet. A bronze light glows on cottonwood saplings and faded roses, lending a mellow warmth to the evening.

Halfway across earth, that light is creeping above the horizon of Thailand, burning mist from rice paddies and glaring white on the muddy hides of buffalo plodding to the fields. In the town of Selaphum, not far from Laos, the monks of Wat Ming Muang stand single file, black bowls in hand, ready to receive offerings of rice and fish from the villagers.

I smile. For me, the image is a pleasant memory. For Tawee Mahaweero, it represents a way of life. About two decades ago, at age twelve, he left his family to serve as a novice at a nearby temple. Eight years later he ordained as a monk, dropping the family name of Thichai and adopting the surname chosen by his abbot: Mahaweero, one who has courage. An apt name, I think, for a man who left his family and then his land and journeyed to a place where coyotes still howl.

Brave Tawee has noticed my smile. He puts down his drink. "What you think about?"

"Selaphum."

He nods, and we are quiet again. Out on the highway, a semi truck labors past, carrying a modern Texas cowboy. In Thailand, that's what people always thought when I mentioned home; "Texas cowboy, pow pow!" they'd say, fingers extended as mock guns.

A year ago, Tawee and I traveled together to Selaphum and the village of Nok Hor, his boyhood home. They are a few miles apart in Roi Et Province on Thailand's northeastern plain, a dry, stark region the Thais call Isaan. Isaan folk are different from other Thais. Heavily influenced by their Lao neighbors, yet stubbornly Thai, they share a language, culture and cuisine unique to their region, and they are fiercely loyal to their rural homeland, where love of family and community are prominent virtues. Even in Bangkok, Isaan folk band together, keeping their traditions alive and insulating themselves from the chaos of the urban center— much like the Washington, D.C., barbeques arranged by and for estranged Texans.

Tawee rarely talks about Isaan, but being separated from it must tear at the center of his being. He left it twice: Once to attend a Bangkok university, pursuing a bachelor's degree in Pali, the sacred language of Buddhism, and again to counsel refugees in Texas. Fate must have known an Isaan childhood prepared Tawee to survive where life is measured against its own hard myths, and in a way it was Isaan itself that brought him to the Lone Star State. A Thai abbot already in Texas wrote Thailand, asking for monks to help the state's Lao refugees. An abbot in Bangkok suggested Tawee, whose Isaan background ensured he spoke Lao. And Tawee, wanting to attend to the religious needs of others and longing to see the world, agreed to go.

That was five years ago. Now, more than 6,000 Lao refugees have settled in North Texas. They are a race with no home, forced by war and an ideological regime to flee their country. Most left behind the possessions, and all, the landscape that defined their lives. Tawee's task is to provide these people with something familiar, a sense of themselves, a place to belong—the very things that make other Texans Texan.

Today, though, that work is done, and Tawee can relax until sunset, when evening chants and meditation begin. He scans the Texas landscape. It looks like Isaan: mostly flat, but punctuated by slight hills and low-growing trees. We are on the prairie, northeast of Fort Worth, just outside the city of Keller, at a place called Wat Buddharatanaram, the Garden Where the Buddha Dwells. It is a temple founded in the early 1980s by Lao refugees and Thai immigrants. More than two-hundred families worship here, and for the time being four Thai monks call it home, each knowing he will return someday to Thailand.

"Maha Tawee," I begin, using a title of respect, "what do you think of when you think of Thailand?"

"How I think of Thailand?" He pauses. "I don't think of place. I think of family: mom, elder sister, brothers and sisters. First year—oh, I am sick for home." He laughs. The whirring of cicada near the temple's pond drones beneath the sound. "Human beings, everybody, know the birthplace that they come from. When we first time leave, it is exciting. Then we think about our birthplace. I close to it for long time, so I love it too much. I think the same for everybody."

Life at Wat Buddharatanaram echoes life inside a Thai temple, even as life outside the wat is curiously different from the Texas wheelin' and dealin' in nearby Dallas and Fort Worth. Each morning at dawn, the monks chant and share a simple meal. They spend the morning studying or in meditation. At eleven o'clock, they eat their final meal of the day, dutifully prepared by Lao women whose families live in the temple complex. Afternoons are devoted to various tasks: cleaning the temple, building a new kitchen, planting flowers and receiving visitors. Each night, the monks chant and meditate again. On holy days, or when invited by a layperson, they perform centuries-old Buddhist ceremonies.

The routine is comforting, but it cannot relieve the anxiety accompanying each trip beyond the temple gate. Tawee lives in a divided world: Inside and Outside. In Thailand, the distinction is one of locale; in America, it is one of opposing cultures. Monks are governed by two-hundred-twenty-seven rules of conduct.

Thai people mature knowing women cannot touch monks, monks cannot wear laymen's clothing and that ordinary people must be respectful of those wearing the saffron robe. That awareness makes life Outside simple: monks in Thailand can ride the bus or take a taxi, attend university classes or walk through the market without worrying about their spiritual purity. In America, all that changes. People stare and point. Women casually brush against a monk's robes. Some laugh at the shaved heads. What we don't understand is that a simple act on our part could require lengthy purification for the monk. In America, a monk must always be alert to an unintentional affront to his status and purity.

"Most American people know monks not well," Tawee explains. "Outside, it is harmful for me. I must have a companion to go outside."

"Doesn't it bother you not to be able to leave alone?" I ask.

"What will be, will be," he says. "First time, I worry. Now I know myself. I know this place. I control my mind. No trouble."

Buddhist philosophy builds on its four noble truths: Everyone suffers in this life; suffering is caused by worldly desire; desire fades if wisdom observes the mind and guides right actions; and wisdom, and thereby true happiness, sprouts from the Buddha's teachings. The goal is to be ever mindful, observing the world but not becoming entangled in it.

"I control my mind. It is calm," Tawee continues. "Look inside. Don't let mind wandering. When it is wander, we suffer."

We stop talking again. Across the field, beyond the pond, Lao children play volleyball with a melon-sized wicker ball. The temple is quiet. A warm breeze lifts my hair. We both are relaxed.

"Tawee? What place is most home to you?"

"Most Home?"

"Where are you most comfortable, most you. What place feels right?"

He leans back and closes his eyes. He smiles gently.

"After we see everything, every place, every people, we can compare. And really, we love our birthplace. Birthplace is really my home—Isaan. Other place different, not home."

He leans toward me slightly, as if he's about to tell a secret.

"But who control mind, everywhere the same. They know to practice in mind to adapt themself to different place, different people, different culture. By controlling my mind, I can adapt myself. When we are good people, we can stay everywhere. The world is house for good people. Sky is like roof. Land, or earth, is like floor."

"Not every person is good," I counter.

"Yes. Some are bad. But all people want to be good, in their heart. I believe in virtue. When we have virtue inside mind we can see everywhere like home. There is no problem. You should consider."

The silence between us is easy as I think about what he's just said.

Finally, I reply. "We learn virtue by controlling and developing the mind, knowing the Buddha?"

"Yes. All people can know Buddha. Buddha is everywhere." He taps a forefinger against his chest, where his heart is pumping. "Because Buddha is here, inside everyone. It depends on the peace and purity of the mind to find out."

Aunt-Irene-and-Uncle-George

JAN SEALE

Their names are a seven-syllable word
always said by the family as one.
He took her back to the cap rock,
the only place in Texas that's neat
on the map—a square—
and put her on a hill beside his Mobile station
and tractor repair shop because he thought
that was what you did with a wife.

The wind had already roared through his ears
20 years and the river 7 miles over and down
had burned deep wordless quicksands in his eyes.
There wasn't any wheat harvest in his blood—
he was born with greasy fingernails—
so he built his shop and pastured
old Studebakers and Ford pickups
out back and down a long gully
and stayed on the land.

Meanwhile, she took the little curly-headed girl
he'd spawned in the war once
when he was on leave and had lived all over with
until '45,
and straight-headed little girl that came
because they were so glad the war was over,
and made-do in the two-room stucco house
he built for them.

She went down the road every morning
and nursed her sick mother-in-law
in the old homesteader's house with red shutters
behind the athel row, and stayed on
to cook dinner for the hands during wheat harvest—
fried chicken, squash, fresh snapped beans,
and always gravy and mashed potatoes
(her brother-in-law had a thing for chicken wings,
and she had to watch or he'd cuss in front of the girls
if anybody got his) and for dessert—cherry pie
she picked the cherries for in Evaline and Claude's
wild thicket.

At night, when the kitchen was put away,
and without a crumb if you didn't want roaches,
they lay down and heard the wind making love to the wires
and a car or two making love to the pavement
and the coyotes taking over the whole moonlit hill for their own.
sometimes there was a possum or a snake in the chickens
and some nights they forgot to turn off the windmill,
and the tank would be bleeding down
that clear cold cap rock wonder water
all over the girls' swing set next morning.
Some nights a car'd stop out at the shop
and he'd raise up when she punched him
and he'd wait five minutes for them to go away
before he'd get up and climb in his pants
and half lace up his work boots and struggle out the door
running his hand through his hair across the dirt yard
straining to see if it was a neighbor needing some gas
for town or just some crazy kids broke down and scared,
and she'd wait barefoot in the crack of the door,
remembering but not letting herself
how he'd taught her to load and shoot the gun.

And the years were a whole long wind blowing the buffalo grass
and the wheat and the tails of the cows grazing toward the river.

And through it all there was a big garden
and good close neighbors just five miles away

and snowstorms when they said
somebody knocked down the fence
between Amarillo and the north pole

and the men came and paved the yard of the shop
with Orange Crush and Hire's Root Beer caps

and he worked on anything that ran up and down the road
for 50 miles around including all the heavy stuff
they brought in to build the dam

and the telephone company came and replaced
all the glass insulators in the line
with plastic gadgets and stuffed
Aunt-Irene's-and-Uncle-George's dump with enough
aqua insulators snarled in line to choke
every prairie dog hole in Hemphill County.

But then, all of a sudden,
the girls were through at Blue Ridge School
and had to go over the cap rock and down to the river
30 miles to school. She told him she thought
she'd move into town with them—
and besides she'd been lonely for 14 years—
but that didn't seem right to him
to do the wind like that

so he built her a first-class house
closer to the road.
She said okay she'd just put her deep freeze
and all her canning jars and Christmas decorations
in the little stucco one
and live like a lady for a change.

And to keep her even happier
he moved the garden
to a new spot to get rid of the nematodes
and quit going to the shop
in the middle of the night
and started keeping his books on paper
instead of in his head.

so for another ten years
she played the piano for their church
of 34 members
and he took up the offering
and gave the Sunday School report.

Then all of a sudden, the curly-headed one
got married and had four of her own
and the straight-headed one
went to be a missionary in Rhodesia.

And now, even though Aunt Irene
has a standing appointment
and sells vitamin products

and Uncle George knocked down his shop
and swept up all the bottle caps
and built a fine new one
right on the same foundation

and even though they both went to Rhodesia
on a vacation

and even though he's a certified meteorologist
so can say before they go to bed any given night
if the good Lord is going to try
to call them home that night in a storm
that will scrape that new shop
and the little house and the big house
off the wheat plain
like an International Harvester gone berserk:

even though all this,
they still lie down at night in their
40-year-long Aunt-Irene-and-Uncle-George name
and listen to that wind making love to them,
telling them who they are, who they are,
saying it so sweet like all the rest
of the world wishes it had only one long name
and knew what to do with 13 inherited acres
out on the cap rock.

The Best Time

JOYCE GIBSON ROACH

I kept up with all that business with Saddam Hussein—Sodamn Insane, that's what the boys all call him when we get together down at the cafe. I was glad they put all that stuff on the TV set so we could see it live and know for sure how it was over there. Watching them missiles whiz in and all them folks putting on gas masks and such was real. When you have to wait and read all that business in history books, you just don't get the whole picture. You have to talk with the people who've been there like those interviews with the troops to find out the whole story. Let me tell you some real history.

I grew up right here. I never left like a lot of other folks did—to make something of themselves, that's what they said. I knew the promised land was right here in Toad, Texas. In Toad, December 7, 1941—now, of course, we call it Pearl Harbor Day—that day meant the end of the Depression and the beginning of lots of excitement. The Depression was a dandy affair. Almost anyone can tell you when the Great Deparession began—1929.

That's when the government, who was a great noticer of things after they happened, said it began. Nobody had anything but nobody had more of nothing than anybody else did and so we all had plenty. There was a long time with nothing much to do, either, but when the war started everybody was hustling and bustling around to contribute to the war effort. Yessir, things really picked up in Toad once the war started. That's why it came as a shock to me when I learned about the bad side of war. Luckily, living in the promised land, I was spared that bit of truth for awhile. You see, we didn't have this here instant, on-the-spot TV coverage then, so how I saw the big war was how my family looked at it and how the town reacted to it.

Like I was saying, during the first part of the war, my family didn't have much money which was a blessing, my mother said, because nobody else in town had any money either.

My grandmother—we called her Mama Hartman—she lived with us during the war. She moved out on the Santa Fe train, and I remember it was quite a sight when we went down to greet her. It looked like she had brought everything she owned, including her mattress. My mother like to died over the mattress part, but Mama Hartman said she wasn't about to leave such a valuable piece of bedding, which was filled with cotton she had picked herself when she was just a girl. She had a feather bed, too, which was ticking stuffed with down and which you slept either under or on top of, according to your choosing. I've still got that feather bed to this day.

We've all got to grow up sometime. It seems to me as I look back on it that I got it out of the way the year I was eleven years old—1942—two years into WW II. Because of Mama Hartman, I was sleeping on the floor on a quilt pallet in the living room, which I didn't mind at all. When the weather got a little warmer, Mother would move it out on the porch, since that was my favorite place to live.

My daddy was butchering beef at the grocery store. He was the only man left in the county with a permit to butcher. Mother spent her time in the kitchen. Mama Hartman was down on her knees most of the time, asking God to smite the heathen and save her boys, Uncle Glen and Uncle Freddie. My Uncle Glen, the Odessa oilfield giant, was chasing a fox named Rommel in Africa. Uncle

Freddie who had just got out of college at Rice was in a big boat, the U.S.S. Blackhawk, taking troops ashore at Iwo Jima, among other things that sailors had to do. I guess our family was lucky, since all the soldiers from Toad were in the Caballo County National Guard, and their unit—Battery F, 131 Field Artillery—was lost; the Lost Battalion. Still, the town wasn't too upset about it. A lot of those boys had stayed lost half the time when they were home and riding fence for the big ranchers in the county. Lost was hardly gone forever—and no news was good news. So, up to 1942, war felt pretty fun and safe in Toad, Texas. Both uncles had been gone since the first year of the war.

As the war went on, the things we did varied depending on who your folks and friends were. The citizens of Toad were having parades or war rallies; saving coupons for sugar, hosiery and tires; collecting tinfoil; buying U.S. Savings bonds to help lick the Axis and giving the V for victory sign. I was aiming to be a cowboy, and practiced every day so I could ride fence for one of the big ranchers when I grew up, which is exactly what I ended up doing all my life. Well, not riding fence, but doing other ranch work. My sisters went into music. They got together with another girl, dressed up like the Andrew Sisters and sang "Boogie Woogie Bugle Boy from Company C," "Don't Sit Under the Apple Tree With Anyone Else But Me," and stuff like that. They got the names of soldiers who weren't from Toad and became pen pals with them. They figured if everyone from our town was lost, they weren't obligated to write to them.

We all saved tin foil from our wrappers which we bought at the Saturday movies. I got to go every week then instead of just once a month like before because they had the newsreels from the war. Mama Hartman complained about Hoppy and Gene, but she really learned to hate Roy singing "In-my-adobe-hacienda-there's-a-touch-of-Mexico-cactus-lovelier-than-orchids-blooming-on-the-patio." She was only willing to put up with it and go with me because she got to see the Pathe news of the war. She always looked for Uncle Glen and Uncle Freddie, but her pleasure was in not spotting them on the screen. It was just the opposite for me. I wanted to see them awful bad because I didn't really know what they were doing overseas.

Some candy was wrapped in foil and we all ate more of it than usual. The war was a pure miracle for allowing me to do more of what I wasn't supposed to. Nearly every rule about sweets was badly bent if not broken. Mother would give me an extra nickel to spend at the movie to buy her something wrapped in tinfoil, so we could peel it off together when I got home. See, first you'd wad a little bitty piece of foil. Then you'd begin to put the other pieces around that until you had a great big old ball. As I would hold one in my hands, I'd think of the bullets and bombs that would grow from that metal and kill the enemy. Oh, don't think I didn't know who the enemy was. Every night I got down on my knees with my grandmother and prayed that God would stop those "boot stomping Germans and those runty Japs." God knew what was what and who was who, and he was on our side.

Like I said before, my daddy in those days had a grocery store and he did all the butchering for the meat market. He was too old and had too many children to go to war, but he'd taken the physical and kept his bag packed by the front door, in case the call should come. Anyway, almost every Sunday after church, where we prayed that God would smite the heathen, Daddy and I would go to somebody's ranch, choose a cow, shoot him or knock him in the head, string him up over a tree limb and butcher the daylights out of him. I liked to see how easily the hide pulled off an old, dead cow and how neatly all the entrails came spilling out in a pile on a canvas sheet spread out on the ground. The rest was just a matter of hacking and sawing and it was all done.

Sometimes the old Indian man, Mama'nte, met us and took all the leavings, hide and all, back to his place south of town down by Toad Gap. Sometimes daddy let me go back to Mama'nte's place all Sunday afternoon, where I'd have fun riding horseback or trying to rope chickens afoot. Mama'nte told me that when I could catch the rooster, then I could start on jackrabbits. Of course, he was only kidding me, but by the time I figured it out I was already one hell of a roper.

Of course, I was just a kid during World War II but as the war progressed, I picked up on the feeling around town that we were still all in it together, me, my family, and the town. But there was a choking feeling, an atmosphere like summer dust, that settled over the town and especially over my own home.

Since all the local soldiers were in the Lost Battalion, nobody ever heard anything about them. We assumed that nobody had died, since no one in town was receiving the telegrams we heard folks in other places were getting. On the other hand, we couldn't assume all the boys were still alive either. The newsreels got worse, showing places like Africa where tanks rolled across desert country that looked a lot like where we lived. And we could see plain as anything that tanks were being blown up. Uncle Glen was in Africa, and Mama Hartman had never gotten a letter from him. The newsreels also showed boats firing guns so big that the movie screen trembled and shook, or at least I thought it did. Mother said it was the cameras that took the pictures that were shaking, not the screen, but it didn't make any difference to me what caused it. And the airplanes! They were taking off from some of the boats and landing on them, too. They were chasing each other in the sky and dropping bombs, and the newsreels showed them so close up, I felt like I could reach out my hand and touch them. Pathe showed other stuff too—people hungry and scared and even dead—dead soldiers. That didn't bother me at first, since the reels never showed dead Americans, but I began to think it over again when Mama Hartman started crying every time we went. She said if those people were dying, then our boys were dying too. She said the government just wasn't showing what all was happening to our boys.

When we weren't going to the movies along with everyone else in town, we were listening to the radio. We had a big old box thing and lots of people along Archer Street came to our house to listen. It was the radio that give us word about the big battles on land and sea, and we began to realize we weren't winning all of them. The newsmen even said how many soldiers we were losing, although they never gave names. Mother and her lady friends rolled bandages, wrote letters and did such other stuff as the Red Cross said needed doing.

All in all, we kept doing the things we always did, but now we weren't so happy and jolly about it. Mama Hartman finally got a couple of letters from Uncle Glen and several from Freddie. Fred wrote a paragraph just to me in a letter and he made it sound like he was having a whale of a time in the Navy. The letters all got to us a long time from the time they were sent, and lots of lines were missing—just blank spaces. Mama Hartman cried like her heart would break and so did my mother, since Freddie was her baby brother, the youngest in the family, just like I was. I cried too, not for Freddie, but for my mother. Everybody that came by cried with us and we went to their houses and cried. And we started holding on to one another. It didn't matter if we were kids. In fact, I think we got held on to more than the grown ups. All the touching and clinging to each other was a new thing to me, but I suppose it helped everybody alot or else everybody would have quit it.

Along toward the end of 1944, Mama Hartman got a telegram. It didn't turn out to be anything bad, but she went all to pieces anyway. The telegram was from Freddie and it said he was stateside and would reach Toad on Friday, December third. Uncle Fred was coming home in time for Christmas! Right then, I believed in miraculous coincidences. I took it as a sign, insofar as my understanding of signs went.

The whole family went wild. In fact, so did the whole town. Mama Hartman and mother cooked for three solid days. The house was scrubbed hard and so was I. Daddy and me went out to the Crosswinds ranch and butchered a Hereford and one of their hogs to boot. On the way back, we stopped at Audie Weir's and picked up three sacks of pecans and cut a cedar tree.

Friday came. Morning passed into afternoon; then afternoon into evening. Finally, Mother and the rest stopped holding their breaths. The phone quit ringing. Neighbors and friends went home from lining the entire street from the square to our house, from the bus station and the train station. Night came on. I had stood the entire day at the edge of the yard next to the road. I didn't move even when the full moon was rising. My stomach was grinding from not eating all day, but the only movement I made was to sit down instead of standing. Daddy came out and said for me to come on in, but Mother called to him to leave me be. The lights were going out in my own house and all the others in the neighborhood, but still I sat staring hard down the moonlit road.

I dozed with my head resting on my knees, my arms wrapped around them, and dreamed or thought I did. What must have been a car door slamming somewhere in the distance brought me awake. Car lights were moving away from the road by the time my eyes were clearing. I thought I heard footsteps and I strained my eyes and ears for a sign. There appeared in the distant moonlight the figure of a man wearing a dark Navy uniform, the gold buttons plainly visible and the emblem on his hat shining. I flew down the bright road, only to stop short in front of him. It wasn't my Uncle Freddie, who had dark hair and stood straight and tall. This man had white hair and he was leaning on a cane.

But then something about the way he stood and held his shoulders told me that it was my uncle. He bent down and asked sadly, in a voice not his own, if I wanted a piggy back ride. There had never been a need for me to think about exactly what kind of a man my uncle was until now, when I saw the man he wasn't any more. I knew without being told that he must have participated in dark and bloody deeds. If his hair color and walk had changed, no telling what else was different.

He started to bend down to pick me up, but I stopped him. I locked my arms around his waist and just started crying.

"I'm glad you're here to meet me and not the others. I need to be with another man now," he said. Then he did just what we'd all been doing at home all along—holding on to each other. I held on to him back.

"But what have you been doing over there, overseas? You never told us. We looked and looked at the newsreels, but you never once wrote and said what it was you were doing." I blurted it out, kid like, the thing that had been on my mind, my family's mind, the town's mind, but had never been said.

"I ... I went fishing alot. I was on the water. I took some men ashore from the big ship in a smaller boat and landed them at a place called Iwo Jima. Then I'd go back and get more and more ... and more. And then I'd go fishing."

I knew he was saying what he thought I wanted to hear and what he thought it best for me to hear. Then the porch lights came on at the house. Mama Hartman and Mother and Daddy and my sisters just swarmed all over Uncle Freddie. Then the women went to the kitchen and started grabbing everything in the icebox and putting it on the stove. And it wasn't long before every light on Archer Street was on and every single neighbor was in the front yard. And pretty soon the fire alarm went off and so far as I could tell everybody in town was at our house. A little after that Old Mama'nte came in on horseback. Uncle Freddie was glad to see them all, but he never let go of my hand, not once, even while I was eating a full Sunday dinner in the middle of the night.

SHELTERS

*R*ooms in a house, an office, a trailer house, the movie theater, the midway, a museum, buildings and landscape—shelters all—provide sanctuary, a place to be, security. **Ernestine Sewell** touches the reader with descriptions of the room within a structure, the kitchen. She provides a bibliography for further reading. **Paul K. Conner**, clear sighted and clinical, speaks of a doctor's office, his office, which has been his anchor. The room never changed, but his attitudes toward the profession and himself have. **James Ward Lee** in a short story writes of the sanctuary of a trailer in the woods and of the comforts Grady Dell found there. A poet, **Tony Clark**, who grew up in a small, rural town writes of the influence of structures on his life and the decisions which had to be made while standing right in front of them. Larger structures which house the artifacts and art of history and culture remind **Frances Mayhugh Holden** that life is a kaleidoscope turning and gathering new impressions, wider visions, with every revolution. **Everett Fly** addresses the subject of architecture itself, the history that attaches itself to buildings and the landscape where people also find place.

...in the kitchen

ERNESTINE SEWELL

The constant factor that imbues youth with a sense of place may well be not so much in John Ericson's arid plains whence comes a chorus of coyotes singing their national anthem, William A. Owen's stubborn soil, Clay Reynold's Main Street, John Graves's limestone ledge, Robert Flynn's Wanderer Springs, or A. C. Greene's personal country, as it is in—of all things—Mama's Kitchen.

The kitchen is perhaps the commonest common denominator for hosts of folks when they embark upon nostalgic trips—whether in their BMW's or their armchairs—to the place that shaped them into who and what they are. Now this is no paean of praise for the long-suffering woman bending over a rude hearth to stir a pot of squirrel stew—Philip Wiley's attack on momism and, more recently, the feminist movement have left the subject of mothers declassé, to say the least. Rather, let's have kudos for the kitchen!

The kitchen Wade Cameron takes his new bride Bethany to, in Loula Grace Erdman's *The Edge of Time*, is part of the one room of his dugout. A homemade bed in one end; a stove, rough table and few chairs in the kitchen end. No cupboards for dishes, no shelves. The dirt walls afford no support for nails close to the stove for pot lifters, aprons, or a calendar. "At home" she recalls, "the kitchen calendar was always covered with cryptic notes" (59), diaries that reflected family activities as their lives ebbed and flowed in and about the kitchen. Bethany determines to be cheerful about her kitchen, but first Wade must devise a way to hang the calendar. It signifies human control of activities that link the family to civilization.

Given a few good years, the pioneer family on the plains moved to a sod house, then perhaps to a log house, and finally to a frame structure. This house marked coming up in the world, and the kitchen would in all likelihood be the one Daisy Hearn Atkins remembers in *'Way Back Yonder*. It was a place where the family "ate, read, studied, fussed, and entertained" (5):

> Our house was on a slope ... we stepped down into the kitchen—it was a long shed room; at one end was the bath room ... a long zinc tub set on a platform with a frame; the water was heated in a wash boiler on the cook stove and carried to the tub.... Water was piped into the house; there was a sink and cupboard below. O! what a wonderful convenience—we thought. Water [for cooking] was heated in an iron tea kettle. Big iron pots were used for boiling—these were always in use—filled with beef, ham, corned beef, beans, cabbage or anything that was edible; waiting for someone who might come in hungry.
>
> On the walls hung many calendars for decoration—as well as to tell the year, month and day—the most important was the McLean's almanac, which gave us the changes of weather—it was seldom right.
>
> There was a pantry too, with a flour bin holding fifty pounds of flour, besides room for a mixing bowl and rolling pin, and twenty-five pounds of corn meal ...(25)

The Atkins family had what seems a typical late nineteenth-century pioneer kitchen. It isn't, however, the pots and pans and trappings that make "Place" of "Kitchen"; it is, rather, what goes on where people break bread together. The Atkins' kitchen was a place for family, friends, and even strangers from along the road to gather, to spend congenial times together swapping stories, exchanging views, finding comfort in the food and each other. This bonding happens even when the kitchen becomes the scene of crisis. In Hart Stilwell's *Uncovered Wagon*, the Old Man, enraged that he should be given biscuits that looked to be made with baking powder instead of soda, runs outside, sharpens his ax, beats on the house, screaming, "G__ d__ baking powder biscuits.... If you want to poison me, why don't you put strychnine in my food?" (5) He reenters the house brandishing the ax, threatening to kill the "poor little ones" (10) whom he swears he'll not leave orphans. All this time, the mother sits calmly, soothing away the children's fears, assuring them the Old Man is not going to hurt them, enclosing the least one in the folds of her skirt. "Her mission was to save us from starvation and our father," (13) Stilwell writes. The stalwart, enduring woman, investing herself in the domesticity the kitchen exacted to fulfill her mission, made of her kitchen a sanctuary.

Or the kitchen may function as civilizing agent when civilization is lacking. "Morning round here," says Augustus in *Lonesome Dove*, "is ... like a nightmare." Despite his attempts to be orderly, coffee grounds are spilled in the grease where bacon and eggs are frying. He fries the eggs "hard as marbles" to compensate for the coffee grounds, but the sizzling in the skillet fails to drown the noise of Pea Eye and Dish standing on the porch splattering the yard. Augustus remonstrates: "It's poor table manners [to perform your morning ablutions] in hearing of those at the table.... You two are grown men. What would your mothers think?" (56) The kitchen, even in Lonesome Dove, is a place where folks are expected to observe at least a modicum of decency and etiquette.

The kitchen functioned in a multitude of other ways. It was the dispensary. Near the water—bucket or tap—was a medicine chest with a good supply of patent medicines and home remedies: castor oil, salts, Cardui, Mustian liniment (good for man or beast), camphor, SSS tonic, alum, asafetida, and a bottle of Bust Head (whiskey, if you will) for medicinal purposes only. Were there a sunny spot, a bucket of aloe vera was kept growing for everything that ailed a body. Drops of boiled onions mixed with tobacco juice cured earache; a drink made with crushed eggshells stopped bedwetting; an onion carried in the pocket prevented fits. Herb teas settled the stomach if Mama took care after the tea was downed, to turn the glass upside down and put it under the bed. (Old Devil Sickness would hop out of the bed, go under it with the glass to get some of the tea, and the sick patient was left recovered.)

The kitchen was a way station for moral and social control, the place where homely virtues were absorbed (and translated into Protestant fundamentalism in Texas). Many, if not most, homes kept a Bible nearby to have morning readings before breakfast. And every child learned to return thanks and was applauded even if the grace came out garbled, as, "Thank you for this food which we are bowed to eat in your many blessings. Amen."

High-toned people sitting stiffly on horsehair sofas in their parlors or relaxing in wicker rockers on their verandas excepted, the kitchen was the entertainment center. There were hard cold biscuits for wheels on little homemade play carts. Flour mixed with water for pasting tear-outs or cutouts. Potatoes for carving. Beans for playing jacks or for filling bags for throwing. Tea leaves for telling fortunes. Corn cobs and shucks for making dolls. Shelling peas made time for telling stories. And grown-up ladies, come to visit, spelled the time gossiping over tea cakes.

A continuity of generations emerged from the easy, relaxed banter that went on among the folk who came together where the coffee was kept piping hot all day on a back burner. Anxieties faded—or were held at bay—against the backdrop of familiar things: the cobbler's box pushed into a corner when not needed. The rack for guns near the back door. The wooden bowl for mixing biscuits, hollowed out by hand by some Tennessee forebear. And the big skillet to put in the little skillet when company comes! Familiar also was the kitchen wisdom for nurturing the young 'uns, the time-honored homilies—call them "mommilies" (a term coined by Michelle Slung in her book by that name). "My Mama dun 'tol me when I was in knee-pants"—or bloomers as the case may be—makes the point. The elders had a barrelful of pithy little sayings handed down from kitchen to kitchen that had passed into the accepted lore of the community. Some were meant to help the children grow and the family stay well; others to protect, to civilize, to teach some personal truth, though it sounds like superstition.

"Don't drink coffee or you will turn black behind the ears," the little ones were told. "If you swallow watermelon seeds, you will have vines growing out your ears." No doubt the children were set to wondering when they heard their mothers whispering about some woman whose belly was about to burst, "She must have swallowed a pumpkin seed!" "Eat all the food on your plate; remember the starving Chinese" was a lesson in compassion as well as frugality. "Don't eat mustard or your feet will stink" was enough to cause one to develop distaste for that condiment. It did, in fact, have a bad reputation. When a boy or girl refused to eat what was placed before him or her, the saying was, "Help yourself to the mustard!" It reminded them of a tale told round tables in Arkansas, Texas, and probably elsewhere among pioneering types. A traveler comes to a log cabin or a stagecoach stop expecting to eat. He sits down to the dinner afforded him. The host has placed a platter of salt pork before him. "I can't eat this greasy stuff," he complains. "Try these," his host says. The traveler looks at the plate of beans swimming in their juice. "I can't eat these beans. Had some yestiddy." "Try this," says the host again, and hands him a portion of ash corn pone along with a pitcher of molasses. The traveler turns away, his face wrinkled with revulsion. "Then," says the irate host, "help yourself to the mustard!" The storyteller reinforced behavior patterns where harsher measures would likely fail.

Because a "stout" boy was a credit to the family, there was meat three times a day. An old-timer who lived to be a hundred had this *remedio* for staying hale and hearty: "Try to get your beef steak three times a day fried in taller. Taller is mighty healing, and there's nothing like it to keep your stummick greased up and in good working order." The boys knew raw eggs were good for everything they needed. The peelings of the potatoes when eaten would grow hair on their chests. Their mamas had encouraged (forced?) them to eat greens long before Popeye discovered spinach made him strong. Once the boys reached puberty, the father dispensed kitchen wisdom. Should the boys be going to town where boxing and wrestling were the street entertainments, he forbade them to eat the rabbit stew that bubbled in the Dutch oven. For he knew, as did the Indians before him, that to eat the flesh of rabbit would make the boys timid when the fists started to fly.

Let there be no disdain for the education that took place in the kitchen. The nineteenth century sage Henry Adams reports in his autobiography that the first step in his education was at three years of age, becoming aware of himself "sitting on a yellow kitchen floor in strong sunlight ... a lesson in color" (5). It is, however, with the girls that one best sees the kitchen as a learning center. The Queen of the Kitchen suffered anxieties for her daughters beyond those of her Yankee sisters. The War of Northern Aggression destroyed all that was orderly and harmonious for Confederate women, and, strive as they did to feign order, there lingered—and does to this day linger—a fear of an uncharted future for their daughters. Their solution was to rear their daughters to find a good man to marry. So in addition to making sure her girls knew a string bean from hot apple cider, she would say, as she worked away at meal fixin': "Eat these bread crusts. They'll make your hair curly." At the table everyone knew the chicken gizzards would go to the girls' plates, for gizzards make you pretty too. Many a daughter no doubt reached for the gizzard eagerly, for in the privacy of some corner, her mama had told her it would make her have large bosoms. If the unfortunate one had freckles, she would wash her face every morning before 6:00 in buttermilk. Lemon juice lightens freckles and the skin, as do burned crusts of bread. A pale complexion speaks eloquently of fragility and gentility, to which the girl would add a suggestion of flirtatiousness. Such homely wisdom emanating from the kitchen was bound to enable the girl to snare a man *if the dainty one knew how to cook!*

Now it was said that if a girl failed to learn how to cook, she was sent to quilt. Quilters would reverse that statement. However, inasmuch as the way to a man's heart is through his stomach, it would seem that girls would rather cook than quilt. *Panza llena, corazon contento*, Mexicans say: belly full, heart easy. Of course, after the young woman won the man's heart, she must strive to keep him at home. Texans tell a story about a man who left his wife four times and came back every time for a piece of her fresh peach pie.

To avoid that fate worse than death—being an old maid—the girls must never shake the tablecloth out of doors after sunset. And never take the last biscuit or the last piece of pie or cake. And never let a person with a broom sweep beneath their feet. And never eat out of a pan or something ominous will happen on the wedding day.

Until the upward-strivers decided it was just too, too provincial to use the kitchen as a family room, until dens replaced the kitchen architecturally, until the advent of TV's and microwaved dinners, the kitchen was the least likely room in the house to undergo change. Oh, a new model stove might be brought in, but a safe for keeping foodstuffs safe from insects and rodents; plenty of table space for working up the biscuits, rolling them out, and for rendering lard at hog-killing time; a table for family and friends to gather round for meals, for visiting, for studying next day's lessons, and just for idle chatter; a rocking chair near the stove for grandma or grandpa: these remained year in and year out. Despite whatever chaos interrupted the even tenor of their lives, the kitchen maintained for the family a semblance of order. Habits were strong in the kitchen; the routines of life were preserved there. Mrs. Bergson's kitchen in Willa Cather's *O Pioneers!* is such a place with a spanking clean white cloth on the table reserved for eating and a pot of flowers on its center. A wooden rocking chair by the stove invites guests to stay for the delicate little rolls coming from the oven, stuffed with stewed fruits and dusted with sugar. Mrs. Bergson strives to continue the old ways and her "unremitting efforts ... had done a great deal to keep the family from disintegrating morally and getting careless in their ways" (28).

"Place opens a door to the mind," Eudora Welty writes, and "[there is] a blessing of being located—contained," because "place connects us with the deep and running vein, eternal and consistent and everywhere purely itself—that feeds and is fed by the human understanding" (Appel, 125, 7). So much the better for those whose sense of place is rooted in the kitchen. Though they depart for distant lands, the bonds forged in the familiar warmth of that kitchen remain; and they may even be heard to murmur at times with some longing in the voice: "Dry bread at home is better than roast beef abroad"!

NOTES

Adams, Henry. *The Education of Henry Adams.* New York: Modern Library, Random House, 1931 (1918).

Appel, Alfred, Jr. *A Season of Dreams: The Fiction of Eudora Welty.* Baton Rouge: Louisiana State University Press, 1965.

Atkins, Daisy Hearn. *'Way Back Yonder.* El Paso, Texas: Guynes Printing Co., 1958.

Cather, Willa. *O Pioneers!* Cambridge: Riverside Press, Sentry Edition, 1962.

Erdman, Loula Grace. *The Edge of Time.* Fort Worth: Texas Christian University Press, 1988 (1950).

McMurtry, Larry. *Lonesome Dove.* New York: Simon and Schuster, 1985.

Stilwell, Hart. *Uncovered Wagon.* Dallas: Texas Monthly Press, 1985 (1947).

The Office

PAUL K. CONNER, M.D.

*B*ecause I am a person, I belong in several settings such as skiing, fishing, hunting, cooking and these activities have offered enjoyment and relaxation and have measured who I was privately. Because I am a physician, I fit comfortably in such places as a hospital, an operating room, a laboratory. These places speak for what I am professionally. But as to my sense of place, none of the settings previously mentioned accommodate me. The place where I belong is my office.

My office represents me on two levels, one metaphorically as the place that houses my credentials—my office-ship—and the other a place where a doctor privately consults with a patient in strictest confidence. The second definition is almost sacred to those who are patients or at least it used to be. All the mysteries of medicine and the possibilities of cure and restoration reside there. Many physicians leave the office as merely a place and go on to home or other places they count as sanctuary. It occurs to me that my office is home and harbor for me. It is the place where I have plied my trade, grown, changed while watching changes in the medical profession itself and come, finally, to a full realization about who I am and want to be as contrasted with who I was and did not want to be. My office and the work that goes on in it represents that location where I am most comfortable, competent and where I feel appropriate. In that setting I also remember, reflect and look forward.

I was reared in Jacksboro, Texas and have beautiful memories of that childhood. Most of my adult life has been spent in Dallas, Texas. I have observed other rural-origined people looking for solutions in the city and city folks looking to the country. These may be called "geographical cures" and are seldom curative. Happily, I have enjoyed living both in the rural and the urban scene.

I spent many of my early years seeking comfort in a niche where I felt that I truly belonged. I seem to have an inherent curiosity about disease and have spent many years in training and equipping myself to deal with disease as a physician. But the style of training in that day attempted to teach disassociation of self from things that were not understood. I became well trained as a physician and would go to any length to make the right medical decision and prescribe the proper medication. My decisions were influenced only by the medical data such as fever, blood pressure, laboratory studies, and such. The boundaries of this type of medical practice that I attempted to engage in initially became too restrictive, and I did not feel a deep relationship with my patients. The relationship seemed very sterile and clinical; however, some physicians would hold that as a proper posture for a healer.

On one occasion I remember reviewing a case with an esteemed professor who upon my mentioning the patient's depressed state told me to disregard it and understand that "life is tough." This is how I was taught to deal with emotions. Then I recognized that I was attempting to isolate the medical from the emotional and spiritual aspects of the patient and discard all but the frustration, but I came to enjoy the feelings of a controlling person whose game plan seemed to be working and from all appearances this endeavor was successful and quite ego-serving.

Also early in my career I had to close my office when a patient died. The involvement I experienced as a result of this sort of endeavor caused perplexing grief. I have since come to believe that I perceived myself as almost god-like. I had feelings of defeat and inadequacy and feelings of competition with disease—sometimes with a war-like demeanor. This led to an ever-expanding ego, and control issues surfaced that almost carried me under. I thought it my responsibility to develop myself as fully as possible, which may be correct, but at one point I was believing my own B.S. and believing in my omnipotence. This seemed to place me above the patient rather than as an equal. Perhaps the recent fabulous expansion of knowledge and technology of medicine led to this. I held the highest rank in my office and firmly believed in the metaphorical representation of the place. I was the office.

Then I became disenchanted with the practice and perhaps burned out. Something was missing. I never really felt fulfilled at the end of the day. I wrote an illegible hand on prescriptions as inscrutable doctors are supposed to do but I came to feel illegible even to myself.

In the confines of my office setting, I began to let go of myself, my ego and my training. It was mysterious and science is supposed to be exact, but both disease and cures are sometimes mysterious. I set about developing a practice from my office in which I could alter the boundaries of traditional medical care of that day. I attempted to deal with the patient in his environment and understand his relationship to his family and others. In internal medicine there is often long term and repeated contact with the patients, and gradually I recognized my way of doing things had been self-serving and not always satisfying and effective for the patient. I can remember early in my professional career I was trained as a consultant but even then I didn't derive satisfaction from seeing a patient and dictating a letter to the referring physician and perhaps never seeing the patient again. The repeated and the enduring relationships became the most important aspect of the medical practice for me. I began to hate disease as disease sometimes disrupted these relationships. Sometimes I almost considered it a personal affront for one of my patients to become seriously ill. But that was when I was playing god.

The opportunities that I have been given to influence some people's lives have been wonderful. As I have matured in the profession it has been these relationships that have been the most satisfying to me, that is, to not only understand their symptoms but to attempt to understand their feelings as well. Early on I kept lists of patient's charts with interesting diseases and problems, but these lists have long ago disappeared and my recall has become my patient, Lucy Smith, with high blood pressure rather than a case of high blood pressure named Lucy Smith.

It seems to me that I have experienced a gradual awakening and awareness of my responsibility in the physician-patient equation, and as such have become a more valuable resource for the patient. There has been a redefinition of my professional responsibilities and emotional discovery of a new sense of trust and a feeling of faith which I have never experienced before. The spiritual seems to have replaced a lot of fear and free-floating anxiety that I had carried in my life. These changes have enabled me to offer a deeper relationship or at least a quality of relationship that was not available to me before.

Many times I find myself discussing fears and anxieties and relationship problems with the patient rather than the symptoms which brought them to the office. Some doctors might consider this non-productive time; however, I consider it cherished time. More and more I am seeing these sessions as very revealing and rewarding. The only limitation in this process is the time it takes. It is truly amazing how by knowing the emotional circumstances of a patient a physician may rapidly focus on a spectrum of diagnostic possibilities because he comprehends the emotional background of the patient. It is impossible to separate a patient's emotions and his illness and to deal with only one aspect of the problem. It took me a long time to learn that.

Unfortunately with the impending power of Medicare and other third party providers this physician-patient relationship as I know it is probably doomed. The tremendous and increasing cost of medical treatment undoubtedly results from technological advances and inflation, plus significant abuse of the system by providers of care who would have you believe that their services are super valuable and who have learned to "play the game" with third party payors. Where this scenario will go, I don't know, but I do accept that this method almost assures the demise of the primary care provider as I know him.

Changes—in the profession, in methods and medication, in attitudes, and in myself. I have observed them all in and from my office. Changes of the sort that I have described and envision may eventually dictate the loss of my sense of place, but because of a place, a room, I have developed a sense of self which has become portable and therefore as secure as the office.

Tubby's Trailer

JAMES WARD LEE

Grady Dell almost always stopped at the last house on his route and visited his eighty-year-old mother for ten or fifteen minutes before heading for the Post Office in Bodark Springs to check in. Today he hoped to get away without seeing his mother, so he quickly pulled out the two letters for Flora and Henry's copy of the *Progressive Farmer* and slid them in the opened mail box. As he started to ease out of the ditch beside the mail box, he heard Henry's voice.

"Grady! Ho, Grady. Hold up a minute."

In his haste to slip away and avoid seeing anyone, Grady had not looked across the road toward the barn, and he had failed to see his older brother bearing down on him. Henry was wearing worn-out 401 overalls and a heavy Oshkosh B'Gosh jumper and carrying two rabbits by the ears. He carried his rifle across his shoulder formally, the way a soldier would.

"Wasn't you gonna stop and see Mammy? You know she could die any day. Hell, Grady, she's eighty—or she will be this summer. And she's done had two strokes, and you know what they say?"

"About what?"

"About strokes. The third one kills you they say. So you ain't coming in?"

"No, not today. I'm running late. I guess I better get on in to the Post Office and check up."

"Get away from here so you can run by Tubby Wallace's to get you a drink of whiskey? Is that what the hurry is?"

Grady blushed. That was what he planned to do. It was what he did every day. He had been stopping by Tubby's trailer house to get a water glass half full of Four Roses every day since August of 1936, the month and year he got so far into debt that he lost his house and had to move Mammy and the kids upstairs over the pressing shop in Bodark.

But he lied to Henry. "No, I ain't going by Tubby Wallace's. I told you I'm running late. Melvin's after me to get my outgoing mail in before 3:00. He likes to get it down to the station so he can knock off at 5:00. Did you ever see it this cold in January?"

Grady wanted Henry off the subject of Tubby Wallace, who was sitting in a warm trailer with no telling how many gallons of bootlegged blended whiskey just six miles out of Bodark on the Highway to Bonham. Grady sighed when Henry opened the door on the passenger side of Grady's new 1938 Chevrolet and climbed in, the dead rabbits now in his right hand and the gun leaned against the front fender of the car.

"Come on, Henry! Don't be dripping blood all over the seats of my new car. I ain't had it two weeks and you know it."

"I ain't gonna get blood on your seats. Them rabbits is nearly froze stiff from being carried a mile in the weather. But if you want to talk about the weather, I've seen it colder in January. Lots of times." But Henry wouldn't have let his younger brother make the weather a topic of conversation if it had been twenty below zero. He looked over at Grady and said, "Mammy's worried about you. Says you look worse and worse every time you come in the house. More hangdog, she says. I thing its more hangover, but I don't say nothing about hangovers to Mammy. Lon Marshall said the other day that you looked like you had been shot at and missed and shit at and hit."

"Lon Marshall is a sorry bastard, one of the sorriest bastards in Texas."

Henry nodded his head, "Yeah, he's sorry all right. But he ain't far from wrong about you. You're what? Forty-seven, forty-eight now?"

"Forty-seven. I'm still just ten years younger than you. You ought be able to keep track of that."

"You've drunk so damn much rotgut whiskey that you look ten years older. You know that?"

Grady Dell sighed. Henry was right, but he wouldn't have taken such talk from anybody but Henry, who had a right to say it. Taking care of their mother gave him the right. Being head of the family in a part of the world where family meant a great deal gave him the right.

"What do you plan to do, drink yourself to death before you're fifty?"

"I take a little drink once in a while, but I just do it to steady my nerves."

"You ought to have 'em pretty steady now from what I hear."

"Goddamit, Henry—" but Grady remembered the bed Henry and his wife Flora had put up in the living room of their two-room unpainted shack so Mammy could have their room. He said in a quieter voice, "I don't have to drink, you know. I don't just lay drunk all the time. I mean I just take a drink once in a while to steady—"

"Yeah, I know. Just to steady your nerves. Was your nerves steady last Saturday night when you and T.J. offered to whip the house up at the Moon River Beach?"

"Who told you that?" Grady was startled to find out that Henry was getting the honky tonk gossip. He thought Henry and Flora lived too far out in the country to hear such talk.

"It don't matter who told me. What matters is that you and T.J. could have both got yourself killed offering to whip them tie hackers and timber haulers from up on the Red River. What was it about?"

"It wasn't nothing. Look, Henry, tell Mammy I'll stop by tomorrow. I got to get on now. Melvin likes to get the mail over to—"

"Yeah, I know, Grady. He likes to get it over to the T&P. I'm sorry I was so hard on you. You come on by tomorrow." Henry opened the door and got out. Then he leaned back in and said,

"Damn, Grady, since Benjamin Harrison died last year, you're the only brother I got. And Mammy won't be with us long. I can tell. I just don't want you to get in trouble. Well, I mean—. Aw, hell you know."

Grady had his head bowed over the steering wheel, looking down at the odometer of his car and reading the 1,200 miles that it showed. Henry climbed out of the car and looked up at a sky as grey as pig iron and as rough looking. Grady leaned across the seat, looked up at Henry, and said, "Wait a minute, Henry. I know how it looks, but I'm gonna get a hold of myself. It's just that— I don't know—everything seems to happen at once, and if it ain't one thing, it's another. You know?"

Henry closed the door and leaned in, "Yeah, I know, Grady, just be careful. That's all I ask."

Grady said, "I will." Then he rolled up the window, started the car, and pulled out into the frozen ruts.

When Grady Dell reached State Highway 5, he turned West and "headed for the barn." The barn was the new WPA-built post office in Bodark Springs, the county seat of Eastis County, Texas. Grady Dell knew every back road north of 5 in Eastis and Fannin Counties and most of the unpaved pig trails in the top halves of both Lamar and Red River. He had ridden them horseback when he was a teenager hunting and fishing along the Red. Then, as a young man, he had courted in a buggy all over the top half of Northeast Texas. Now, as a mail carrier, he put in 30,000 miles a year hauling mail over the back roads of half of Eastis County and half of Fannin. And he estimated that he still put in 4,000 to 5,000 night miles a year hitting all the honky tonks on both sides of the Red. Grady did all his driving north of the T&P and Highway 5. For a reason he could never quite figure out, he didn't much like to go south of State 5 and the T&P line. Those two arteries—or maybe they were veins—bled Northeast Texas. The merchants along the twin roads saw them as highways bringing in goods to be sold. But Grady thought of the roads as escape routes for the young. Every kid that he had seen grow up for nearly twenty years—ever since he had come back from the War in 1919— couldn't wait to set out for Dallas to make a fortune or get into trouble. Or both. Nobody seemed willing to stay in country villages like English or Telephone or Ravenna or Novice, and most weren't even satisfied with small cities like Honey Grove, Bonham, and Bodark. Somehow Grady couldn't really imagine living anywhere but in Eastis County—or Fannin maybe. And Grady had seen New York, London, Paris, and Brussels. The song that said, "How're you gonna keep 'em down on the farm after they've seen Paree" didn't apply to Grady Dell. He no longer hunted and fished the river bottoms of the Red and the Sulphur, but he knew he could if he wanted to. For Grady, everything north of the T&P seemed new and fresh and washed clean, even when it wouldn't rain for two months and the roads got so dusty that a small wind would blind you with red dirt as you drove along. Even when the Red River was dry enough to plow, Grady had a feeling that it was washing the country. He could sit in his car in the heat of August and look down the bank above the dwindling stream—hardly big enough to call a river—and think that the "Old Red" was washing Fannin and Eastis and Red River Counties clean. And in some way Grady thought the dirty river was washing him clean too, taking his weakness for beer and whiskey and women down the stream to wherever it was that the Red went. Was it the Mississippi? Or was it the Gulf of Mexico? He always meant to ask his daughter Jackie to look it up for him in school, but he seemed always to forget.

Grady had a funny feeling about those parts of the Red River counties south of the T&P and Highway 5. The people seemed different, the land softer and more worn. The Black Waxy Prairies ran south of the twin roads, and the people down there had more money and an easier living. North of 82 was hardscrabble country. Up north, if you made a dollar, it came the hard way—from hacking ties or row-cropping or making a little white whiskey. You grew your food or you shot it or you fished for it. You didn't buy much of it at the grocery store. These were the people that Grady had grown up with, and he understood them better than he did the town folks and the more prosperous farmers in the south halves of "his" counties. Or so Grady thought. He never made a run that he didn't think on the people and the place.

Grady dreaded the thought of driving up to the post office and lugging his sacks and the undelivered C.O.D. parcels in. He hated the look he always got from Melvin Spruill, the postmaster appointed when FDR became president. He liked Joe Hurst better—even if Joe was a Republican. Joe had been postmaster all through Harding and Coolidge and Hoover. Grady started when Wilson was president. Melvin was postmaster then, but was turned out two years later when Harding beat Cox. Joe Hurst was a friendly man who could take a drink and laugh when you said something funny, but Melvin was dour and dry. He gloried in Prohibition when it was the law in America, and even after FDR, his president, got the law repealed, he did what he could to keep Texas dry. He couldn't manage all of the state's 254 counties, but he was working hard to do his part with Eastis, though the "wets" were talking local option again.

Grady knew Melvin had noted his hangover this morning when he got to the post office to sort his mail. And he knew Melvin would be watching him this afternoon to see if he had been by Tubby's. Grady thought, if the damned preachers and bootleggers didn't run this damned county, a man could get a drink and not have to pay three prices for a shot of Four Roses. Melvin and his bunch of damned church-goers were making Tubby Wallace rich. No telling how much money Tubby paid the "drys" in the last election, which they won three to one. Damn, Grady thought, I'll never live to see it so a feller can get a bottle of beer in this county. Then he laughed to himself. He got all the beer he wanted. There must have been twenty honky tonks scattered across the piney woods of Northeast Texas that would sell you a bottle of Oklahoma 3.2 beer. You could sit there and drink it at the table as pretty as you pleased even though it was against the law. Hell, these honky tonks were making Sheriff Herman Wells rich. There was an old saying in Texas, "all you need to be a millionaire in Texas is to serve one term as sheriff of a dry county."

Grady drove west on Highway 5 at a steady 40 miles an hour, looking off the south at the stubble of cotton fields frozen solid in this hard freeze. The sheets of water that had frozen in the fields looked like mirrors under the dead-gray sky. Grady tried to take an interest in the landscape, but his mind kept returning to how warm it would be in Tubby's trailer house and how warm the Four Roses would be in his stomach when Tubby poured him a "big shot" in the back room that he had partitioned off for sit-down drinkers. Not that Grady was a sit-down drinker. He usually stepped behind the partition and stood there as Tubby poured the glass a little more than half full for Grady. Then Grady would take his left hand and hold his nose with it while he picked up the glass in his right hand and drained the contents in one long gasping swallow. Then with a shudder and a strangle, Grady would set the glass down and pay Tubby the dollar that he charged for a double shot.

Tubby was always generous to Grady, for they were veterans of the same war. Grady had gone over as an infantryman with the 1st Division, and Tubby had been a machine gunner with the Rainbow Division. Their outfits fought side by side across France, and both Tubby and Grady had been gassed when the Germans got desperate in 1918. Tubby Wallace was a hero who had "got shot all to pieces" at St Mihiel. That was one reason Herman Wells left him alone to sell bootleg whiskey. But that was only one reason. The other was that Tubby paid Herman about ten percent of what he made to stay in business. Grady had been a hero too, but he had kept quiet about his part in whipping the Kaiser. Grady and Clint Murdock from Tennessee had wiped out a machine gun nest in the Argonne Forest and his corporal said that made it possible for the Eighteenth Infantry to get out of the woods alive. Grady's regiment went into the Argonne commanded by a colonel and had been led out by a corporal. That's how bad his war had been. But Grady had no medals except for the Crois de Guerre that the whole First Division got from France. Nor did he want any. Grady mostly wanted to forget the war and those ten German children that he and Clint had killed before they knew what they were doing. Grady and Clint went in with fixed bayonets and rifles blazing. They shot seven and Grady bayonetted two before saw that the dead weren't grown men. They were fifteen-year-old boys who froze in terror as the Yanks leapt into the machine gun nest. Clint had just stabbed the tenth German when Grady saw what they had done and said, "Oh, my God in Heaven, Clint, look who we've killed!"

Grady never got over it, but Clint was killed the next day by a sixty-year-old German grocer from Koblenz who got off a lucky shot.

These were the thoughts that always ran through Grady's head as he got close to the cut-off that led to Tubby's trailer. As he turned up the rutted road that led to Tubby's, he always stopped thinking about the war and began to worry that somebody might see him as he went in to get his drink. There must not have been three grown-ups in Eastis County who didn't know that Grady was drinking all the time now, but he fooled himself that he only drank a little and that hardly anybody knew. It was against the rules for a government employee to drink on the job, and Grady had almost led himself to believe that since he had delivered the last piece of mail he was legally or theoretically—or at least "in the sight of God"—off the job. But he wasn't. And he knew it.

Grady hoped every time he pulled into Tubby's clearing that all he would see was Tubby's 1937 La Salle coupe sitting under the big hackberry next to the trailer. Tubby had the finest car in Eastis County. It was a La Salle "doctor's car," and even Doc Clayton didn't have one of those. Clayton had as much money as Tubby, but he thought it would look bad to drive anything better than a Buick. Tubby always said, "Well, I 'spect I practice about as much medicine as old Doc Clayton, so it's only right for me to have a 'doctor's car.'"

Today, Tubby's car sat alone. Grady breathed a sigh of relief as he pulled in beside the big V8. He got out of his new '38 Ford for the first time since he had left the post office in the morning, groaned, stretched, and hobbled up to Tubby's door. Tubby had seen him coming, so as soon as Grady raised his hand to knock, Tubby hollered, "Come on in, Grady. You gonna freeze out there in this weather."

Grady stepped inside the door and limped toward the coal stove that Tubby had sitting in the middle of the room. "How come you limping, Grady? You didn't fall down last Saturday night up at the Moon River Beach, did you?"

"Damn, Tubby, does everybody in the county know every move I make?"

"Might near. After all, everybody knows you, being as you're the mail carrier and all. What's really the matter with that leg?"

"It's just gone to sleep. Does it everyday. I guess I sit in one spot too long. I probably ought to stop and walk around once in a while, but I don't usually stop till I get to Henry's."

"You seen Dr. Clayton about it?"

"Naw, Tubby, it usually goes away when I walk around a little."

Tubby rocked back on the legs of the straight chair he sat in and said, "Your mama had a stroke, didn't she?"

"Yeah, she's had two," Grady mumbled. Then in a clear voice he said, "You saving that whiskey you got in the back room for something, or do you think you might like to sell somebody a drink of it?"

Tubby heaved his 300 pounds out of the chair and headed for the "back room." Grady followed. Tubby scrabbled around in a trunk and came out with a quart of Four Roses. Then he reached up on a shelf and took down a barrel-shaped water glass that weighed half-a-pound and filled it three-fourths full for Grady. He set it on the table. Grady reached for it—and for his nose at the same moment—and drank it off in one long, choking swallow.

After Grady had shuddered and put the glass back on the table, Tubby said, "I God, I wouldn't take on like that if I was to drink carbolic of acid."

"Me neither if it was carbolic acid, but that rotgut you sell is worse than any acid. But bad or good, it'll give me enough kick to get through the rest of this freezing day."

"Grady, about that leg of yours—"

"Now, Tubby, there ain't nothing wrong with my leg. It just goes to sleep when I set in the car all day."

"Does it stay numb after it wakes up?"

"Aw, it tingles a little bit most of the time, but it ain't nothing to worry about. If I didn't sit all day long it wouldn't always go to sleep. Besides, cold as it is now, everybody tingles some."

"Well, Grady, I ain't no doctor, but I ain't no damn fool either, and if it was me, I'd see Clayton about it. You might be fixing to have a stroke like your mamma."

"Naw, I'm all right. What do I owe you?"

"Same as always—a dollar."

"You poured her pretty full today. I thought you might be running me a dollar-and-a-quarter drink."

"You looked like you needed a little something extra. Besides, us old vets got to stick together."

Grady put his hat on and opened the door, "I appreciate it, Tubby. I'll see you in a day or two I expect."

"Hell, Grady, you'll see me tomorrow," Tubby said after Grady had closed the door.

Grady Dell felt like a new man now that all four of the roses were flushing his cheeks and kicking his circulation to life. His leg had lost most if its tingle, and he thought he might be able to face Mammy and the kids if he could get by Melvin and Charlie Stone, the window clerk. Both were churchgoers and hard-case prohibitionists.

Well, it won't be long now, Grady thought. Tubby was just four miles outside Bodark Springs. Easy driving distance for the thirsty, but far enough away to be out of sight of the town's churchwomen. Grady made it to the edge of town in eight minutes, and as he turned onto the courthouse square, he took a package of Sen Sens out of his shirt pocket and popped two into his mouth. Then he eased the car into his slot on the side of the post office. He sat there with the car running and thought about his mother and Henry and his brother Benjamin Harrison, who had died last year, and about his father, who was killed in 1921 when the mules ran away with the wagon he and Uncle Leo were driving from Honey Grove up to Monkstown. He thought about his own ruined life and about the German boys he and Clint had killed 1918. His leg didn't hurt anymore. But somehow he couldn't reach up to turn off the switch key. He thought, I'll turn it off in a minute. Then he said out loud but in a voice that only he could hear, "I wish I had a little drink to steady my nerves. Then I'd be all right and could turn off this car and go check up."

While Grady sat with the motor running, Henry's old 1927 Chevy with the eisenglass side curtains pulled into the spot on Grady's passenger side. Henry got out and tapped on the window and motioned for Grady to roll it down. When Grady didn't move Henry opened the door.

"I hope he don't have them damn bleedin' rabbits," Grady said in that same voice that only he could hear.

"Grady, are you all right?" Henry leaned in closer, but Grady didn't move.

"Grady, it's about Mammy. Grady, are you too goddamned drunk to turn your head? I said Mammy had that third stroke and died just after you left to go to Tubby's. Yeah, I know you went there because I stopped off in that goddamned trailer and asked Tubby was you by there. He didn't want to tell me, but when I told him Mammy was dead, he said, 'Yeah, Henry, Grady was by and you'd better get him to see old Clayton. He don't look good to me.'"

Grady sat staring ahead thinking about how warm it was in Tubby's and how much he needed just one of Tubby's "little shots," just a third of a glass of Four Roses.

"Grady, is something wrong? You couldn't of heard about Mammy. Did you? Are you sick or something? You can't be so drunk you can't move. Why don't you turn off that motor?"

When Henry reached out to shake Grady, his younger brother slumped against the driver's door and sat silent. Henry couldn't hear Grady say, "Here. Wait. Just gimme a minute. I'll be all right. All I need is a minute to rest. If I had another little drink to steady my nerves, I could see about Mammy."

The Day Gene Went Up Against Bambi

TONY CLARK

No decision was lightly made
If it involved Gene Autry.
Eight-year-olds in Dallas
Were spared such dilemmas:
At their neighborhood Roxie
They took what they could get.

But my small Texas town
Boasted—on the same side
Of the square—two theaters
Whose flashing facades reared
Like temples of conflicting faiths:
The Mecca and The Jack.

My mother let me out
In No-Man's-Land, surrounded
By the bigger kids' parked bikes
And there I stood alone
Grappling with my conscience
While wringing my quarter.

Gene saw me first:
His white hat dazzled
From the lurid poster
And his too-perfect teeth
Smiled like a pal: old loyalties
Had me leaning toward Mecca.

But I was pinned down, caught
In a crossfire of paper gazes,
Because welling teardrops of eyes
Were pleading with me
From the poster of forest flames
That flared outside The Jack.

Clearly Bambi, frozen in the fire,
Was counting on me. But I was burning!
Must a choice between virtues
Reduce at last to a sin?
Do deep-felt affections,
Pledged in joy and for nothing,

Have to wind up in chains?
Choking back sobs,
I dashed blindly to the booth
And cast my lot with Bambi.
    After that first time
It was always easier.

The Devil in Fort Worth, Texas

TONY CLARK

We had started out in darkness
aboard the FFA bus with bad shocks
and jostled through January cold
to arrive at the Fat Stock Show
With extra cash and eyes wide open.

After passing a required half-hour
checking Brangus and Santa Gertrudis
in the manure-ripe cattle barns,
Coley and I made a beeline
for the flash and dazzle of the midway.

The gray sky sagged with ice,
but swirling light shredded the chill
and lost it amid the oily noise
of popcorn, free-wheeling metal
and a meld of many musics.

For weeks we'd dreamed of the rides
and were headed for the Tilt-a Whirl
when a voice like prairie fire
came flashing across the sawdust,
compelling us to a peppermint awning:

"Yeah, you," he flared again,
"the one in the turd-colored coat!
Here's where you win a solid gold watch."
His leer from behind the counter
fixed us in a hell-red glare.

Behind him, the shiny prizes stood
like stars on rows of sticks.
Wanting against our wills,
we inched closer—for these
were not pandas or plaster dolls

but heavy treasures of hard metal:
watches, yes, and man-sized rings
with eyes like rubies and opals,
cufflinks the size of limes,
and, high on the farthest tier,

a rank of gleaming pistols.
"What's the deal here?" Coley said,
surly because of the insult
to his new leather jacket
but lured by lust for a German Lugar.

"Knew ya was a sport," the carny taunted,
his grinning face engorged with rage.
He hacked a tobacco glob over the rail
and wiped juice from chin prickles
with the greasy sleeve of his shirt.

Lurching out, he clattered a fistful
of wooden rings against Coley's chest.
"Ya just toss wunna these-here hoops
over wunna them-there prizes,"
he said, "and it's yours for keeps!"

When he winked and leaned closer,
his whisky-reek made the air close
and us nervous. Coley turned to me
as if to leave, and spoke in stone:
"I bet they're only fakes, anyway."

"Hey, son," the carny shouted, like
nobody's father ever, "son, if them
ain't real guns that'll shoot
real bullets and kill real people,
then God's a possum!"

His speech cost Coley fifty cents,
but it scared the bejesus
out of me—being schooled in stern
Jehovah and the fire next time,
I knew a lightning bolt should strike.

While I trembled and Coley took
his chance, the carny kept right on
grinning: the sky didn't part,
the earth held firm. For me,
Because of that cold day in hell

when blasphemy was allowed to live,
God will never be quite the same.
It's a measure of His magnitude
that He can encompass possum, fish
and dove, as well as rattlesnake.

Kaleidoscope

FRANCES MAYHUGH HOLDEN

*M*emories, often comforting, but sometimes tragic, evocative and elusive, are tangible evidence of living, preserved in the kingdoms of our minds in the form of a kaleidoscope, a finely crafted cylinder, turning, whirling and capturing, again and again, patterns of time, place and people which have colored our lives.

The process of preserving the records of other people, whether through their cultural artifacts or their recollections, is like looking through a kaleidoscope, too. One turns the chamber to witness the wide variety of people and locales falling into their various perspectives. When the circle is completed, the new starting place may be familiar, but the trip is ever fresh and exciting as old landmarks merge with new.

From a girlhood and growing up on three sections within Colonel C. C. Slaughter's giant Running Water Ranch, to field trips to Mexico, to the Sonoran desert among the Yaqui Indians, to the museums in Santa Fe filled with Spanish treasures, to the museums of Europe and the Middle East, to a marriage with Dr.

W. C. Holden, Professor of History and Anthropology and Director of the Museum at Texas Technological College in Lubbock, I have vivid memories of the people, their arts, crafts, customs, celebrations, entertainment, architecture, archaeology and landscape. I recognized, had vision enough to know, that all those elements of culture ought to be preserved, recorded and captured to identify a sense of Southwest place for all time. Vision combined with perseverance has been a life-long labor for Curry and me.

Curry was a born builder as well as a born teacher and leader of men—and women. He loved building the Museum at Texas Tech, from the basement unit in 1936 to the two story L-shaped building completed in 1950, which included a "Life on the Plains" gallery, a "Hall of Earth and Man" and an art gallery for changing exhibitions, and a small auditorium. Lacking state funding for exhibits, Curry turned to me as a "Premiere Volunteer" to research and design the galleries and exhibits, to originate programs and publicity, to acquire collections, and to eventually create the Women's Council as support arm for the West Texas Museum Association. And, so I did until 1965, when Curry retired as Director of the Museum. However, in 1970, we both enjoyed generating funds for the $2,500,000 handsome new building for the Museum, moved to a 75 acre plot on the accessible edge of the campus.

More glorious grist for the Southwestern kaleidoscope was the Peter Hurd Mural, begun in 1952 and dedicated in 1954. Painted in true fresco on the circular walls of the 1300 square-foot entrance rotunda, it served as a focal point for the Museum. Peopled by those who found their settling place on this prairie, it is an illuminating portrayal of the flow of life across the Southern High Plains from the 1890s to 1925, when Texas Tech was established.

My trusty kaleidoscope never faltered as I moved my range from Lubbock and West Texas to include the whole state and then the western borderlands as far north as Canada. In the mid-1970s, I had the idea of creating a ranch headquarters, as outdoor museum which is currently known as the Ranching Heritage Center. With the backing of Texas Tech's president and a group of fine, honest-to-goodness ranchers and many other supporters,

Curry and I supervised the development of this assemblage of historic ranch buildings. This visible representation of the ranching industry's heritage truly creates a comfortable feeling of "place" for many Texans, Westerners and international visitors.

Other opportunities were waiting with another turn of the kaleidoscope, however. I had not yet worked with words to preserve history. My book on an early phase of the ranching industry, *Lambshead Before Interwoven, A Texas Range Chronicle, 1848-1878,* was the result of research begun when a friend asked me in 1978, "How could the name Lambs Head [early spelling] be attached to a cattle ranch near Albany, Texas?" I followed the history trail through Clear Fork country in which Lambshead Ranch is situated, thence to Devon, England, from whence came Thomas Lambshead with wife and child in 1847. Ironically, whatever quirk of fate caused the area to be identified with Thomas Lambshead, remains hidden.

I did discover tantalizing facets of the history of Lambshead's range and of the Joseph Beck Matthews and B. W. Reynolds families, who first ranged, then occupied it from the 1860s to the present. In this history-steeped soil, I felt I had found a true "home place," where Curry and I continue to return and to travel the trails with genial host, loyal friend, and mentor for the book, Watt Reynolds Matthews.

Since publication of Curry's novel *Hill of the Rooster* in 1956, his friends have made the rooster his symbol. For my part, I have long collected mermaids because they are a part of my mother's family crest from Scotland. A wrought iron rooster and mermaid ornament the entrance wall of our adobe *casa.* Symbolizing the very close relationship existing between Curry and me since our marriage, this inscription, in Spanish, has been beautifully lettered by a gifted artist friend. Ornamenting a beam are the words "*En la casa del gallo y sirena, el es ella y ella es el.* To the words, "In the house of the rooster and the mermaid, he is she and she is he," might be added that the partners "rooster" and "mermaid" continue to locate their sense of place in the kaleidoscope of cultural rituals of the Texas and Southwestern landscape and to preserve them for others who come after.

Landscape, Buildings & Sense of Place

EVERETT L. FLY

There is no question that many things contribute to the condition known as "sense of place." In most cases only the obvious elements dominate the attention of the traveler or visitor. The prominent features tend to be recalled as unique groupings or associations which define the sense of each physical place. Then there are the intangibles which contribute to the qualities of place. Culture, history, and folklore are a few of the ingredients. The range and type of combinations are endless.

We seem to understand the substance and significance of people and events which determine sense of place. However, the physical environment does not receive the same in depth recognition as a contributing humanities element. Every human event has a backdrop or setting. Santa Anna's surrender to Sam Houston at San Jacinto took place under a tree planted by nature. The Old San Antonio Road (King's Highway) has been used by conquistadors, settlers, slaves, farmers, and tourists for three hundred years. Lyndon Baines Johnson was born in a simple hill country farm house. History is made virtually every time the legislature meets in the State Capitol Building in Austin. The Battle of Flowers Parade has followed various routes through downtown San Antonio for one hundred years.

A place dominated by natural landscape features has an order of its own. Hills, valleys, and mountains are formed over the ages, not over days or months. The life span of these elements is far longer than that of a single human being, or even an entire civilization. The processes which produce oceans, deserts and forests are powerful forces and enormous in size. Temperature, smell, wind, and sound are significant features in natural landscapes.

Landscape designed and built by people combine characteristics and attitudes of their time to produce simplistic imitations of nature. The ideals of the designer, owner, and users are expressed in the final composition. Technology and science allow the new landscape to replicate or abstract natural phenomenon. In other words, culture, society, and history are present in these new places.

In cases where buildings and architecture dominate the setting there is more than meets the eye. Style, materials, color, ornamentation, shape, and scale are obvious parts of a building. Each architectural composition is an expression of the owners, builders, and designers. Not only a technical and formal expression, but a personal and subjective manifestation as well. The construction tools and techniques say as much as the choice of colors and materials. The building is also an expression of its time. Time in the literal sense of date of construction. But inherent in each structure is the technology, theory, values, attitudes and economics of its period.

Texas has a tremendous array of places. The state also enjoys a human history ranging from prehistoric native Americans to current times. Sense of place is a dynamic mixture of people, landscape, buildings, history, and culture. Dallas would not be itself without its downtown skyline, Trinity River, and commercial business interests. East Texas would be unrecognizable without its casual pace of life, pine scent, and the late nineteenth century architecture. El Paso would not be the same without the Franklin Mountains, Juarez, Mexico, and the Rio Grande between.

It may be argued that every spot on earth has a sense of place. One should hesitate the next time a declaration, "this place is no place," is about to be issued. Sense of place is not defined by one piece of land, or one building, nor one group of people. Sense of place is many things to many people at different times. It is physical and spiritual, current and historical, natural and constructed, sensory and perceptive.

RITUALS

Ab Abernethy in The Bounty of Texas *says that "Customs are life's personal patterns." Further, the editor and secretary of the Texas Folklore Society, identifies "personal legends"—those stories that we all tell about ourselves which define who we are—and therefore an individual's sense of place. **Judy Alter** carries the idea further in a short story which testifies to the influence of place in the lives of long ago and which shows how custom and responsibility dictated behavior. The personal patterns observed in building, walking, reading define place for **Jim Harris** as he speaks of Mary, the beloved. **Robert Flynn** addresses another kind of personal myth, the hunt, in short story form, and observes that females do not always understand. The ritual of dance or of a football game transforms feeling into place for poet **Tim Seibles**. **Ab Abernethy** remembers Village Creek as he recreates himself, renews himself, through the act of fishing. Feelings have everything to do with ritual, a prescribed way of doing things. **Lionel Garcia** recalls the sounds of bells in his young life which reminded him of who he was and who everyone else was, too. **Robert Compton** invites us further into the subject of place by offering a bibliography of Texas and Texans.*

Fool Girl

JUDY ALTER

"**J**osie!" Pa's voice boomed out so loud and sudden that I almost dropped my broom.

"Yes, Pa?" I was in no hurry about sticking my head out the door of our dogtrot cabin. Pa always wanted something—a horse's hoof held while he repaired a shoe, someone to carry the other end of a log, someone to curry his two workhorses. Pa should have had ten sons, but he only had me, a fourteen-year-old daughter. Still, I thought I was about as good at most chores as any boy would have been.

"The workhorses are gone!" he thundered, and it's a wonder every Indian from here to the reservation didn't hear him.

Pa had set our cabin square in the middle of the North Texas prairie when he first came home from the War between the States. He was determined to farm, but three years running his luck had been bad and there'd been no crops to speak of, nothing but a small garden that was mostly my doing and kept us in table food of a sort. First it was a hard freeze, then the seed was moldy, and then Ma died and he couldn't work for grief. This was the year he was going to have oats and corn, he told me, and this day he had set his mind to plowing.

"The workhorses are gone," he repeated, mad as he could be at everyone—me, the horses, the world in general. "You'll have to go get 'em."

"Maybe Indians took 'em," I said. If Indians had them, they'd be beyond finding.

"Ain't no sign of Indians," he growled. "Goddamn horses broke the gate and walked away while we slept." It was almost an accusation, as if we shouldn't have slept. "I said you'll have to go get them."

"Yes, Pa." Pa was in one of his moods, and when he got that way, there wasn't much I could do to change him. Ever since Ma died, he just seemed to get stubborner and stubborner. I wanted to ask why he didn't go after them himself—after all, he couldn't plow until he found them—but experience had taught me better than that.

"Don't come home until you've found them," he said.

"What if... what if I can't find them?" I blurted out as a vision rose in my mind of endless days on the prairie looking for two horses too dumb to come home.

"You'll find them," he said grimly and stalked away. "Better take the six-shooter." He threw the words over his shoulder.

Figuring I might be gone long enough to get hungry, I gathered up some corn dodgers from breakfast in a clean handkerchief, one of Ma's that I treasured. Now it would have grease all over it. And I got the six-shooter off the shelf where Pa kept it. Heaven knows what he thought I'd shoot from horseback with that unwieldy weapon. By the time I got it loaded, any self-respecting Indian would have scalped me and a jackrabbit and would be clear to Oklahoma. But Pa had taught me well, and I knew better than to ride with a loaded six-shooter.

As I got my things together, I thought bitterly that if Ma hadn't died, I wouldn't be goin' out on the prairie. Ma always wanted me to be a lady, and she was the one person Pa never stood up to. When I was younger and he wanted me to ride with him, Ma would say, "Hush, Luther, she's practicing her stitches. A lady must sew neat and fine." I was almost angry at Ma for dying and leaving me.

Outside, I whistled for Maisiebelle, the mustang Pa had given me three years before. He'd been disgusted when I named her, said she needed a short name 'cause she was a short horse. Pa never did like her since she tried to bite him 'fore he even got her home to me. But Maisiebelle and I understood and trusted each other. She was about my only friend living way out alone like we did, and I told her all my hopes and dreams, for all the good it did me.

Pa had waved his arm east, and east was where I headed, pointing Maisiebelle across the vast Texas prairie. We loped along, my eyes scanning the horizon. All I saw was the great empty land covered with rolling prairie grasses and dotted with an occasional clump of mesquite or blackjack oak, treacherous outcroppings of rock, and straggly little creeks, seldom enough for fishing, and sometimes in the hot summer nothing but baked dry earth.

Expecting the horses to materialize out of the land at any moment, I rode straight on, moving at a fairly good clip. In spite of her name, Maisiebelle was all mustang and could go forever. Not, I thought, like those two heavy-footed animals that Pa linked to the plow. At first, the sun was warm and good, and I forgot my anger in the freedom of being out on the prairie, smelling all its good smells, and being away from Pa and his mood.

"Maisiebelle," I said, "we ain't always goin' to live like this. Someday, I'm gonna have me a fine house, a big house with two stories and servants to run up and down the stairs, and I'll wear beautiful gowns, and you'll eat sweet clover all day long." The little mustang nickered, and I knew she understood my dream. Content with the perfect day and my perfect dream, I almost forgot how mad I was at Pa.

But the sun climbed straight overhead, and it turned from warm and good to downright hot. I wiped my sleeve across my face and used the old battered hat I wore to fan myself. Shielding my eyes with my hand, I searched the empty land once again. I could see forever and there were no horses. No men nor houses either. Just emptiness.

What kind of a father, I thought, would send a girl out into such emptiness? He didn't care what happened to me, I told myself. Maybe he hoped I would get lost or Indians would get me—one less thing for him to worry about. But then I straightened—Pa sent me after the horses 'cause he had confidence in me. He just didn't recognize that I was a girl, with a girl's dreams.

When I judged the sun was direct overhead and it must be midday, I nooned, sitting quietly in the shade under Maisiebelle, for there were no trees nearby at that point, not even a scrub oak. It was what cowboys call a dry camp, with no water, and the corn dodgers, now hard and cold, stuck in my throat with nothing to wash them down. I threw the last one on the ground, and even Maisiebelle sniffed disdainfully at it and turned away. I wondered if Pa had warmed the dodgers on the stove and had them with cool buttermilk that had been stored in the crock. For a moment, I wished fiercely that I was back in the dogtrot, Pa's temper and all. But then I moved on.

Even that poor meal made me sleepy, hot as the sun was, and as Maisiebelle, now moving a little more slowly, headed even further east, I nodded in the saddle, overcome by weariness. Two or three times I startled myself awake and looked frantically about the prairie, as though by dozing for seconds I had missed those darn horses. But there was nothing—just me and Maisiebelle and emptiness.

I must have slept soundly however briefly, with the saddle providing a strangely rocking kind of cradle, for this time when I came awake, I did so with great clearness of mind, the fuzzy sleepiness gone. And instantly I knew that I was alone and, though I would not have told Pa, afraid.

"Pa wouldn't have sent you if there was any danger," I lectured myself, unconsciously sitting taller in the saddle. But there was another part of me that didn't believe Pa had even thought about whether or not it was safe.

Loneliness and fright are like a fog. They settle all around you, resting on your shoulders like an invisible cloak, and no matter how you think about it logically, you cannot shake that fog. I lectured myself again and again, and I even shook my shoulders a time or two, as though to chase away that feeling. But I'd find myself checking over my shoulder more and more often as the afternoon wore on.

Ahead of me I could see the Crosstimbers, that irregular, narrow band of trees that stretched up across North Texas to the

Red River and into Oklahoma. The Comanches used the timbers as a hiding place, I knew, especially in times of the full moon when they seemed more prone to raid. Fear clutched at me as I remembered that it was now a full moon, and just two days ago we'd heard of neighbors who'd lost their horses to Comanches. They were lucky, however, for they kept their scalps.

I looked around almost frantically, determined that I'd find those horses before I reached the timbers. I was convinced that once out of the open, into the wood, I'd not only lose the horses, I'd lose myself and likely, I thought, also my scalp.

The sun was well on its way down when I rode within a mile of the first trees, my desperation increasing. There seemed no way I could turn and make it home before the middle of the night. I'd lose my way on the prairie a thousand times. And besides, hadn't Pa said not to come home without the horses? Yet to enter the timbers went beyond anything I was capable of in my wildest imagination. I wished desperately for Pa, unpredictable as he was.

I'd seen not so much as a pile of dung to indicate that the work horses had come this way. Perhaps Pa had been wrong, and they'd gone west and I'd been on a fool's errand all day. Half expecting the horses to be plodding along behind, I turned in the saddle, sort of standing in the stirrups as though that would give me a better view. I did not see two heavy workhorses, but I saw a lone rider coming at a good clip.

He was not Comanche, that much I could tell even from a distance by the way he sat a saddle and the broad hat on his head. I could, of course, have headed quickly into the timbers, for I had plenty of time to beat him and lose myself among the trees. I stopped Maisiebelle and simply sat, waiting for the rider to approach.

Within minutes, I saw that it was Pa. Had he come to harangue me for my failure to find the horses? Would he holler that I was sitting still when I should be pushing on? Common sense told me I should make some last-minute effort to find those horses, dig them out of a hole in the ground if I could, but I sat, frozen, waiting for fate to come to me.

Pa reined his horse to a stop in front of me, raising his hand in the traditional sign of friendship. Then he sat and stared at me, his expression unreadable.

"You've come a good twenty miles," he said. "Why did you come so far?"

Defiantly, I asked, "Why did you tell me not to come home until I found the horses?"

"Fool girl," he muttered, "don't know no better than to ride halfway to hell and gone."

Years later I figured out that was the closest he could come to showing his concern. Then, though, I took it for condemnation and burned under the phrase, "Fool girl."

We rode home together in silence, though Pa did tell me that the workhorses had come home of their own accord, shortly after midday. He never did tell me, though, and it was years before I figured out for myself that two slow workhorses could never have gone as far as my mustang and I had that day.

Josie Parker finished her story and sat silently on a bale of hay, her elbows resting on her knees as she stared at the horizon and a prairie now dotted with fences and building. She was a tall, lean woman, hardened by years of hard work. Today was a working day like any other, and she wore a pair of faded jeans, scuffed boots, a kerchief around her neck, and a battered Stetson.

The young man had come from a city newspaper to interview her. His assignment was to find out how she felt about having spent her life—eighty long years—running a ranch with the help of no man, save her father who had died years before and now the few she hired.

"Why...?" He stumbled over the question. "Why did you want to be a rancher, Miss Parker? Most women of your generation married...or taught school... or..." He was getting himself in trouble and he knew it. "Why did you choose to run your father's ranch?"

She stared at him as though he were a fool. Then she spoke very slowly, "When I was young, I lost two workhorses on the prairie."

Mary, This Place

JIM HARRIS

We build a barn on our two acres
back in the corner away from the house.
There are holes to dig, posts to erect, cement to mix
and sometimes a moment to watch this woman
who spends her leisure day
working with me in the sun.

She pulls the string for setting beams,
she holds the line to make the corners square,
she balances a long level
along the sides of upright,
while I bring in the nails
to hold it all in place.

We stop for water in the afternoon heat
so I can watch her drinking,
her face eager for more work
for the roof that will be ours,
another part of our land's puzzle,
another piece of this place that has chosen us.

*Photos by
Jim Harris*

There Is No Day Better Than This

JIM HARRIS

In the morning in the mountains I read Othello again
for the tenth time or the twentieth time the Moor gets jealous.

In the afternoon in the mountains we walk the sunny slopes
for the tenth time or the twentieth time I get jealous
of the trees and bushes she walks through like a Venetian princess.

She has some words for me while the grass listens while the wind
moves through the pines like a rumor on fire and I wait
for the world to make some other sound It does not
and since I am with her there is no day better than this.

Women Don't Know

ROBERT FLYNN

Yeah, ole Doc. Course he wasn't no real doctor or nothing; if he finished high school that was the best he done. Doc was a plumber, and a good one I bet, although he never talked about it. Martha acted like she was kind of ashamed of it. Women don't admire things like that.

The reason we called him Doc was because him and me was out hunting one time and I saw this nice ten point buck that run before I could get a shot at it and he said, "In five minutes that buck's going to put his head in that little clearing right there." Damn if he didn't and I shot him. Good ten point buck; not a real wide spread but out to his ears and heavy horns.

I said, "How'd you know he was going to do that?" And Doc said, "Smart as I am you ought to call me professor." And damn if he didn't look like a professor with those thick glasses and that kind of hunched over look he had like he was examining something real close. I told that story when we got back to camp but we didn't call him professor, we called him Doc. Everybody but Martha. She called him Harold. Harold, dear. Till the day he died.

She couldn't understand how come we called him Doc, and the first time I told her the story how come she looked at me like I told a bad joke. "That was just luck," she said.

Of course it was luck. Doc didn't know what a buck was going to do no more than anybody else, and besides that he couldn't see. Everybody knew it was luck; that's why we called him Doc. If he really knew where a deer was going to poke his head we wouldn't a called him Doc. We'd a called him Elmer Fudd or Barney Fife, the way we called Wilbur Price "Daniel Boone."

"I wish you'd stop calling him Doc," Martha said, when I asked her what she wanted me to do with the horns off that last buck Doc shot. "Now that he's dead it isn't funny any more." But he'll always be Doc to me. Women don't appreciate things like that.

One time I bought this fake diploma, Doctor of Phunology it said, and hung it in the cabin, and Doc got a bigger kick out of it than anybody. Next time he came out to the lease he was wearing one of them funny flat hats with a tassel like professors wear. Only his was camouflage. If there was one thing ole Doc knew it was how to have fun. He made fun out of everything. It didn't matter who the fun was on.

Doc was scared of snakes, more than anybody I ever saw. All hunters have a respect for snakes because you're always stepping or sitting where a snake might be, but old Doc didn't even like pictures of snakes. Well, I got this little rubber snake and put it in his sleeping bag, and when he felt that snake he come out of that bag—tore the zipper off of it. He hit the floor crawling and rolling and skinning his knees, and laughing cause he already knew I had tricked him but he still couldn't stop until he was clear on the other side of the cabin. And then he just sat there and laughed. "Damn, they make those things real don't they?" he said. He got as big a kick out of that as anybody. But he never did get his bag fixed no matter how cold it got. He was afraid I'd do it again.

Doc couldn't see too good, even with those thick glasses on, so he usually hunted with me so I could help him spot deer. I shot this fourteen pointer one day, horns weren't wide but they had dog-catchers, and Doc walks up where he can see it and he hauls off and kicks it in the ass. "God damn it, I've been looking for that moose for two years," he said. "Well, get back, I'm going to gut the son of a bitch."

But if a deer moved he'd spot it. I pointed out this real nice twelve pointer one time but he couldn't see it until the deer ran, and he gut-shot it. Damn he felt bad about that. We looked for that buck until we found it, but it was dead and the meat wasn't any good. "Well, get the horns and let's go," I told him. It was a wallhanger but Doc wouldn't take the horns. "You just going to leave them laying there?" I asked him. We were right close to the fence so he gets the idea to wire the deer to the fence so the other hunters would see it standing there and shoot it.

He put it behind some brush where you didn't get a real good view of it and propped its head up so it was looking at you and you could see those horns. Nice heavy horns. One of the best bucks I ever saw on this lease. We drove off aways and stopped to see how it looked, and damn if it didn't look good. I started to drive off and Doc says, "Wait a minute, that looks so good I'm going to shoot it myself," and he did, right in the neck where he should have shot it the first time. I think everybody on the lease shot at that deer until somebody finally took the horns.

Ole Doc felt bad about me having to spot for him, so he devised this plan to help me out. I had spotted this real nice buck in Buck Valley but I never could get a shot at it, so Doc told me to climb up over the Turkey Tracks and down into the valley and him and Wilbur Price were going to drive the long way around the road, and they was going to walk in and run that deer out the other end of the valley right by where I was going to be sitting. Wilbur was the sorriest hunter I ever saw. There was a little milk-sucker that we saw every time we left the cabin that nobody else would even shoot at and Wilbur missed it twice.

I got up three hours before daylight, and took my flashlight, and oh it was cold. And rough. I was having to climb over those three hills with a flashlight in one hand and rifle in the other and before I got to the second one my flashlight burned out. I stumbled over rocks and cactus and ran into mesquite and catclaw, and I was all tore up by the time I got to Buck Valley. And sweaty. And course the minute I sat down my seat got cold.

But I got there in time to let everything get quiet around me so the deer would forget I was there, and along about daylight I hear Doc's truck rattling down the road. I'm shivering so I don't know if I can hit anything, but they're coming down the road, so I get ready as best I can. Then I hear this shot, and I hear the truck doors slam, and I can hear them talking. After a while doors slam, the truck starts and they drive away, and I'm yelling, "Doc, Doc, wait for me."

They drive off and leave me. I sit there for a while getting colder and colder and trying to think what to do. Walk a hell of a way around the road or climb back over those three hills. I go back over the hills. I walk into camp and there is Wilbur skinning my deer. And it's better than I thought it was. It's Boone and Crockett. It looks like a damn moose.

I walked into the cabin and there is Doc having lunch. "Hey, did you see that big buck Wilbur killed?" Doc says. I am so mad I can't even speak. Then it dawns on Doc what he did. "You climbed over the Turkey Tracks."

"Twice," I remind him.

"Sit down, I'm going to fix you a sandwich."

"To hell with it. You'd probably forget to put the bread on it," I tell him.

Ole Doc is trying hard not to laugh but I can see his shoulders shaking. "How in the hell did you and Wilbur ever kill a deer?" I asked him. "You can't see and he can't shoot."

"Damn buck was chasing a doe," he said, " and stopped right in front of the truck to look at us, and Wilbur shot it. I got so excited about him finally getting a buck that I just forgot." He just had to laugh then, and I couldn't help it, I laughed too.

"I bet that's the only buck Wilbur ever shoots," I say, and damn if I'm not right. The next day Wilbur comes in, starts unloading his rifle and fires a shot through the cabin. There are three hunters in the cabin and he's such a sorry shot he misses all of them, but the other hunters vote not to ask him back. They don't want him on the lease.

I paid ole Doc back, although I didn't mean to. One year there was this big boar that kept tearing up fences and getting into the oat fields so the rancher hired a man to come in with dogs and kill it, and the boar killed two dogs and put the dog man up a tree. Oh, it was mean. So the rancher hired another man with dogs and asked us hunters if we'd help, and everybody wanted to kill the boar, but I knew Doc didn't have a chance because it would be at night and he wouldn't be able to see it.

So I devised a plan. I see where this hog leaves the oatfield and goes down this draw, and the draw gets deep and narrow at this one point so that if the hog's in there, that's where he's got to stay. So me and Doc dig a hole in that narrow place, and Doc lays down in it, and I tell him, "When that boar hears those dogs he's going to come right through here and he's going to be close enough so you can see him, but for God's sake don't miss." That damn hog was a killer.

Well, Doc lays down, and he waits and he waits. And he has a couple of drinks to stay warm, and he goes to sleep. All of a sudden he hears this racket and looks up and there is the big boar coming right at him. He doesn't even have time to raise his rifle. He just covered his head with his arms and the boar ran down his back and broke two ribs. Ole Doc couldn't laugh because he hurt so, but he said it wasn't the boar running down his back that hurt so much, it was the dogs jumping on his broke ribs.

I took him to the hospital and called Martha, and by the time she got there they knew he didn't have no internal injuries, and when I told her about ole Doc laying there and the hog running down his back I couldn't keep from laughing. But there was no laughter in that woman. Women don't think things like that are funny.

After that she kind of blamed me for everything. But I couldn't stop him from hunting any more than she could. Doc wasn't supposed to drink and he didn't bring anything to the lease, but somebody always had a bottle and he'd usually join in. But nobody drank much any more. Not like the old days. One time Doc ran into town and bought a whole case of champagne.

"What are we celebrating?" we asked. We thought Doc must have shot the moose he was always talking about.

"My turkey," he said. Doc had seen this turkey and shot it and when he went over to pick it up, it was an owl that had caught a mouse. Doc saw that mouse hanging down from the owl's beak and thought it was a turkey beard. We laughed and got drunk and puked all over the cabin. God, it was a mess.

Ole Doc laughed more than anybody about that. Course we didn't tell the rancher, because he would have raised hell about shooting an owl. So would the game warden. We didn't tell Martha either. Women don't understand things like that.

We don't drink like that any more. Too old I guess. I told Martha that. She said, "All I know is, if he'd stayed home he'd be alive now."

Maybe he would have. Maybe he'd a been alive and wished he wasn't. I don't know that, either, but I do know he died doing what he liked best. He was up in the Turkey Tracks and shot a buck and was trying to drag it out by himself. He should a come back and got one of us to help him, but he was proud of himself and he wanted to bring that buck back to camp and show us what he'd done. He'd finally got that moose he was always talking about.

When he didn't come in for lunch we got worried about him and went looking. It was late in the evening when we found him. He was just sitting there, leaned back against that buck like he was waiting for us to find him, waiting for us to see what he had done. He had kind of a smile on his face and he would a been looking at us if the birds hadn't gotten to him first. Damn birds.

Sometimes I wish I'd a been with him when he shot that buck. I'd a helped him drag it out and he'd still be alive. Then I think, Doc didn't want no help. That's why he went off by himself. He wanted to find that deer and shoot it and show it all by himself. I didn't tell Martha that. I didn't tell her about the birds either. That's the first thing a man would'a asked. But women don't want to know things like that, so I didn't tell her. I just told her he was sitting there with the biggest deer he'd ever shot. I didn't mention his eyes at all.

The paper did a story on him and Martha told how he had his own plumbing company, and the clubs and church he belonged to, and how he had been president of the Chamber of Commerce and member of the City Council. That didn't surprise me none, but we didn't talk about things like that. Course I knew he had been in the war—we talked about that and where all we'd been—but I didn't know that he got a medal for putting out a chemical fire and that was why his eyes were so bad. You don't tell friends things like that and ole Doc and me was friends although I only saw him at the hunting lease.

I packed up his gear the way he would have wanted me to and took it to Martha. She took his rifle for her son and she said, "There's two things you can do for me. Stop calling him Doc and burn those old clothes." Course Doc did wear old clothes a wino wouldn't die in, especially that old Navy coat that probably went through the fire with him, but I guess I looked at her kind of funny. "Harold wasn't like that," Martha said. "He was a very successful man. You didn't really know him."

Martha told the paper that he had died hunting, the way he wanted to, which I thought was nice of her to say. She didn't mention his first wife at all, which I thought she should have, Mary being dead and all. And I was surprised that he had a stepson. I don't remember him ever mentioning that.

Martha didn't tell them the most important thing of all. She didn't tell them how good a buck he got. Women don't understand things like that.

Who

TIM SEIBLES

Who doesn't
want to dance
to be inside the body
not somewhere beside it
to feel the arms and legs
hot and clean in a clear lake of air
like fins, as though every limb
were a fish for a moment
free of the water out of the world—
the body, strange as a planet
reeling in its own soft sparkle

Who doesn't want to dance
to let the body go gracefully mad
to fall into the music as though
from a cliff—every muscle a feather
every three feathers a bird every bird
bald blind and falling
as though the fall itself were the dance
as if the music were a cushion of air
a wind holding you up as though
in motion the body is a leaf is a
new fabric better than feathers better than water

Who doesn't want to remember the feet
to wash them in music
to feel gravity's tireless kiss
bringing you back, pulling you in
as if there were only you and the earth
and music were the sea
and the body were a small ship with lungs
as its sails—as though breathing
were dancing and dancing were living
and living were enough. Who doesn't
want to dance?

Nothing But Football (for Melvin Strand)

TIM SEIBLES

I

Brother, those days in the schoolyard
playing football with the sun
preaching heat to the asphalt, when
we thought everywhere was Sharpnack Street—
those were good days: you and me
and all the moves we used, our feet
fast and smart as God, our heads saved
from everything but dreams
of getting the ball and that single
glorious, ever-present possibility of *touchdown*.

II

Our sneaks laced with *NFL Highlights*
Mel, with a football in our hands we were
right as priests: celibate, heaven clearly in sight
ready to abandon the world just to get closer
just to fake the hell out of anyone
trying to stop us. They couldn't stop us—
You stutter-dipped, I snake-slipped, anything
to spin-shimmy away clean as light, slick as sweat
holy thieves in a forest of moving trees: What
hymn, what hidden but unquestionable singing
did we dance to then?

III

I hated to play against you, trying to read
the mystical sermons of your feet, the blur
of your Converse high-tops, that sudden cut that
always came sure as dark, you smooth bastard
and the finishing gallop that left us praying
to your back. There was nothing
more beautiful, no creature more purely one
with its escape, and I have loved nothing
and no one more than that twelfth summer
we roamed the schoolyard beyond our parents
riding a football into this life—every day
a new game. Every catch a blessing.
Every opening, a parting of the sea.

Village Creek

Photo by F. E. Abernethy

Sweet August

FRANCIS EDWARD ABERNETHY

He lay stretched out on an old quilt on the bank of the big creek, head propped on a chunk of wood, reading a paperback western. He was shirtless and barefooted and he dozed off intermittently. When he would ease back into consciousness, he could hear the cicadas singing and the sound of Village Creek rushing over a log near the far bank. The late August afternoon was hot and still and dry on this fringe of the Big Thicket, but it was cool enough for comfort on the shady creek bank.

This was his second day on Village. He had left the city and his college classes as soon as he had turned in his summer semester's grades. He had put his boat in at the highway bridge and motored upstream about a mile before he made camp.

He had waded the creek and fished the afternoon before and had cast every bait he had but had not even gotten a tap. He had the same luck sleeping. He never slept well the first night out. He lay on the ground atop a quilt folded in a piece of canvas, and every rustling armadillo or squawk of a night bird brought him awake and shining his flashlight to see what was out there. He wasn't afraid of the dark or the creatures it held, but he was apprehensive about being startled.

He had counted on a catfish breakfast but his drop lines hadn't been touched. The small-bream bait were white-eyed and bent stiff. After breakfast he had motored up the creek and drifted and fished back to camp, but he still hadn't caught anything. Later he put a small popper on his fly rod and fished a dead-water oxbow that lay in the woods behind him. The four goggle-eyes that he caught and the remains of last night's pork and beans made spare dinner.

Now he lay completely at ease. His teaching job and the city and his responsibilities were lost in a haze somewhere in the dim mid-reaches of his mind. He had slept and read and looked and listened, and he no longer was aware that he had a body with him. Once he watched a rain crow moving furtively through the top of a water oak that towered over him. He watched its body stretch and its throat surge as it rattled its announcement that rain would come—eventually. Two chameleons on a berry vine paraded and displayed their rosy throats with all the miniature mock magnificence of their mighty ancestors of old. He came out of a doze once when little green acorns began to fall as two young cat squirrels picked through the ripening mast, looking for one that was ready to eat.

Around five o'clock he got up and sat on the creek bank and rolled a cigarette. His Protestant ethic urged him to fish. That was the stated purpose of the trip—to fish. But he was content to be just sitting, and his previous luckless excursions failed to motivate or excite him. Nevertheless, after another thirty minutes of sitting and looking and feeling good he got up, cut a chew of Tinsley and waded out into the creek.

This time he fished downstream, which he always felt was bad practice. The water was cool and alive, and he began to get the old feeling of serious purpose that always activated him when he fished or hunted. He started off throwing a green Hula Dancer, then shifted to a black Hawaiian Wiggler, a Tiny Torpedo, and Tandem Spinner, in that order. The Spinner, a last-resort bait, agitated a bed of green sunfish, but he didn't catch a thing, and the sun's light was quickly fading. He sampled a few 'possum grapes growing over the water. He had waded over to them from necessity after throwing the Spinner about two feet deep into the draped vines. He was also backlashing about every third cast. He saw muscadine vines on the bank, and this was his excuse to climb the bank out of the creek, eat a few of the muscadines that had dropped, and head back to camp.

He put on dry pants at the camp and lay down to catch enough of the last light to read, but it was quickly dark. Then he lit his kerosene lamp and hung it on a branch and built his fire up against an old punky log. He boiled some coffee and opened a can of Spam. He had planned to fry the Spam in the meal and flour he brought for the fish but he ate it cold. After dinner he dragged his bed near the fire and positioned the lantern so that between firelight and lamplight he had enough light to read. He fell asleep just as the rising full moon began to show through a crack in the woods and trail a quivering ivory path down the long straight run of water in front of his camp.

He awoke when the moon hung almost overhead but past meridian height and on its way down. The lamp still burned, the fire had gone to embers, and he had a crick in his neck from sleeping with his head on the log pillow. The woods were absolutely quiet. Only the creek flowing over the log made a sound. Except that now he heard another sound in the water, a new sound that grew closer and more distinct as he came awake.

Bass—and they sounded like big bass—were viciously striking in the glassy dark waters of the creek below. The sound was not the single explosive chug of a bass taking a frog or a fish at the top of the water. It was a series of long swooshing sounds with a chop at the end, as if the bass were slashing through a school of fish. He decided that shad or mullet had come up the creek from the Neches River a few miles below and the bass were feasting on a bounty.

He got up and gazed down at the flowing water, shaded from the moonlight by the big trees along the bank, and an excitement seized him. He got a flashlight, harnessed it with a piece of throw line, and hung it around his neck. He got his rod and reel, and after picking through his baits, he tied on a topwater. He waded out into the creek picking his steps timorously in the darkness of the black rushing water. The sound of the striking continued upstream.

He got to the middle of the creek and stood there trying to see and get his bearings. He was tense and shivering in the hot night. He called up his courage and made a long cast into the dark upstream, where the steady slashing strikes could still be heard. He cranked rapidly to keep the bait ahead of the flow of the water, and the first strike was immediate and so vicious that it hurt his rod-holding wrist. He held what he had and started backing frantically toward the bank, when the plug came flying back at him.

He stopped, disappointed, then spent several minutes cranking down to his plug and getting it out of the brush. He waded out and cast again. This time he backlashed and hurriedly snapped on his light and began picking out the snarled line in his reel.

The next cast fell short but the strike came hard. Again he backed toward the bank, this time jerkily cranking against the determined resistance somewhere out in the dark water. He made it to the shelf below the bank and, moving along the shore, finally got the fish on land. He was able to put his foot on it and in the dark reached down and gingerly gripped its lower jaw. He walked up to camp and held it up in the moon- and lamplight. It was a big Kentucky bass, maybe as big as three pounds, closer to two-and-a-half, looking like five.

Carefully he took the fish to where the boat was tied and snapped it on a stringer and trailed it out in the water.

He waded out and cast again. He cast three more times and unsnarled one more backlash before he had another strike, and dragged and cranked him in. It was a match to the first. He hung five more and brought in three of them, all of them near the same size. He stumbled and fell and splashed around and backlashed and got finned and hooked — and pumped adrenalin.

Then it stopped. He kept casting down the black slot of the creek, but the feeding was over, and he caught nothing but brush.

He waded back to the bank and the boat, unsnapped the string of flopping fish and took them up to the light to admire. The five fish were proudly heavy and he laid them down in the light and rolled and smoked a Bugler and admired them.

He finally put them back in the water. Later as he sat around the re-built fire he kept wanting to go down and look at them again, but he didn't. Both pairs of pants were wet now so he stripped down to go to bed. The canvas he pulled over him felt comfortable. He lay wide awake from the excitement, but he watched the moon as it moved on down into the trees again. He finally fell into a deep sleep.

The sun was high and he didn't wake till a pileated woodpecker started hammering on a dead limb almost over him. The chips were flying as the big bird pounded and pried after its breakfast. He got up naked but warm in the morning's sun and walked down to the boat and the bass. They were still there, alive and glisteningly beautiful, a picture to hang on the wall.

He waded out to a patch of warm sunlight, where the water was waist deep, and lay back and floated against the stream's flow with only his heels holding him in place. Then his body, rippling white in the clear water, slowly arced around until the current lifted him and began to float him downstream. He lay on his back, heels bumping softly in the sand, sculling easily with his hands. The trees touched leaves above him and moved upstream, blessing him from head to foot as he passed under them on his way downstream. Out of the corner of his eye he watched a curled willow leaf that floated along with him. Man and water, leaf and loam, bass and bank became one. All of them a natural part of the natural flow of life through the deep woods.

The water got deeper and then shelved off at a long bend till it was over his head. He sank and rolled over and dog-paddled up to the surface of the slow current, barely rippling the water, with just his nose and the top of his head above the surface. He became an alligator and slowly moved his head around, scanning the bank and brush along the bank. Then he gently sank back and downward until his feet touched the sand bottom. He surged forward, moving smoothly under water with the flow. When he came up he hung for a while at the surface and then glided easily over a blackgum log that lay across and just below the surface of the creek. He caught the current again where the creek narrowed and floated and swam and rolled with the flow until he came to another bend with a sandbar inside its curve. He drifted up on the bar and lay in the sun-warmed water on the sloping sand shelf, his head resting on his hands, chin in the water, basking in the shallows.

Then he became a man again and stood up on his hind legs and squeegeed himself off with his fingers. He picked up a stick and strode off along the bank, toward his campfire and canned pork and beans.

An hour later he sat in the boat headed downstream toward the highway bridge and his car. The fish were pulled in and lay at his feet in the bottom of the boat. His chuck box and war bag lay in front of the middle seat. He had on damp pants and his cap and was pleasantly ruminating over a fresh cut of Tinsley.

He could hear the highway three bends before he got to it; it was a cacophonous contrast with the gentle rippling sound of the creek. The bridge and his old '49 Chevy looked different from what they were when he left them, but he knew that his eyes were only seeing differently, probably better. He cut off the gas to his motor and rode a couple of circles, running out the gas in the carburetor. The motor finally died and he coasted in to the landing.

An old man sat on the bank with a couple of lines out in the deep water under the bridge. He watched the shirtless, shoeless fisherman get out and drag the bow of the boat up on the shallow bank.

"Hey there, d'ja do any good?"

The fisherman turned and spit and grinned and said, "I never go that I don't."

Remembrances of Childhood

LIONEL GARCIA

I was born and raised in San Diego, Texas, the county seat of Duval County. The long history of political turmoil has for years covered the little town like a black cloud. It has the reputation of being a bad town. If that were not enough, the more recent publicity brought on by a gang rape has added another layer of agony to its people.

In San Diego's defense I always argue that my parents live there, my in-laws live there, my younger brother and his family live there, most of my childhood friends live there, and they are not bad people. My wife and I visit two or three times a year to be with family and friends, to reminisce.

I walked the dusty streets as a child, barefooted, my pockets full of marbles and a spinning top, looking for a game to play. We were carefree then, getting up in the morning, leaving home after breakfast and not returning until dark, all dirty and sweaty, hoping that some supper had been left for us. As we crossed the yard between my grandmother's house and ours we could hear the voices of our elders as they sat on the porch, my grandmother fanning herself, shedding the intense heat that had consumed her in the kitchen the whole day. Under the stars and amid the sounds of the locusts they would make beautiful talk, about people alive or long dead, and when there was disagreement about a date we would run to get Merce, my insane uncle, who knew the exact date of birth of all the family present and gone.

In his youth he had been sent to the insane asylum in San Antonio and in a short time, according to my grandmother, he had memorized all the streets in the city. If he had a fit during the conversation we would just let him go running through the streets as though nothing had happened. "Be careful," my grandmother would say. "Don't run into anything."

It was easy to laugh and to cry in the dark with the stories.

We were raised with certain traditions that become very meaningful as one grows older. In San Diego, the Spanish priests had brought over the European tradition of communication with the townspeople through the church bell. The good news and the bad were passed on to us by the ringing of the bell as the great poet, John Donne, had so eloquently written in 1624 in his *Devotions upon Emergent Occasions*.

I remember that on Sunday mornings Father Zavala would have us ring the large sonorous bell an hour before the mass, repeated metallic peals that penetrated throughout the sleeping town. Every fifteen minutes he would give the nod and my brother Dickie and I, dressed in our starched red cassocks, wearing shoes for the first time that week, would both hold on to the large rope and tug at it with all our might, the weight of the swinging bell picking us up from the floor on the upswing.

Father Zavala himself would ring the bell to announce death in the little town, the large bell, going on and on, a woeful sound of death that bound the town together. More tragically, the small bell would ring for the death of a child, a lighter, sadder tone announcing the unfairness of life. We would stop to hear the sound, taken from the game of *canicas*, or *trompos*, or *la chusa*, to be reminded of our own mortality. My mother, Marillita, and my grandmother, Maria, would stop the old washing machine. The soulful peals would continue their cry. No words needed to be spoken. We would run barefooted to the church to find Father Zavala resting against the wall, the old man exhausted from ringing the bell. He would straighten up, clear his throat and announce the dead person's name.

Off we'd run back home, our feet burning on the asphalt under the scorching sun, reciting the name over and over to be sure that we would not forget, would not announce the wrong name. One time we did get it wrong and my grandmother cried all afternoon for her favorite cousin until her cousin showed up on foot, asking for a cup of flour. We had to ran away from home for a while after that one.

Regardless of who died, to my grandmother it would always be a relative. It could be a cousin ten times removed on my grandfather's aunt's side but it was always someone she knew. And she would cry, not the wails that she made when my grandfather died but still she cried. And she would get my mother to start crying, both of them trying to clear the tears from their eyes with their soapy hands, feeding the wash into the rollers.

Years before, my grandfather had said that my grandmother Maria should hire out for wakes and funerals to prime the mourners, to keep the wails going.

We'd leave our marbles on the ground and run to the printer, who was by now busy laying type for the *esquelas*, the official announcement of death: the person's name, date of birth and death, family, dates and times for the rosary, funeral. He would soak the printer in the blackest ink that he had, trying to contrast the letters with the gray background, the letters rolling out as black as death.

It was our job to distribute the *esquelas*, holding on to the car door, standing on the runningboard, jumping off the car and running to every screen door in town and slipping the notice on the door handle. We got paid ten cents, fifty if the person was important.

That night Dr. Dunlap would go through town in his car with Clementina, his nurse, sitting by his side, showing him where everyone lived that had called to complain of shortness of breath. Sometimes he had so many people to see that he wouldn't arrive until well after our bedtime and he'd catch us asleep. But we would wake up just to see him. To us it was all a game. To Dr. Dunlap it was work and we killed him with work.

When he took out his magical stethoscope we would all be awed. He didn't have to ask for quiet. You could almost hear my grandmother's heart beat as she sat straight on her large chair like a queen. He would gently place the instrument on my grandmother's chest and move it around once in a while, asking questions of Clementina. Clementina translated them into Spanish. Had she eaten a lot of fried food? No, sir. Never. We would laugh. Everything my grandmother ate had lard in it. How long had she felt bad? Since in the morning when she was kneading the dough for *tortillas* and she had heard the tolling of the bell. Finally, Dr. Dunlap would roll up the stethoscope around his hand and look my grandmother in the eye and tell her that she had the heart of a young woman. What a joy that was. We could go out and play knowing that our grandmother would live to knead more dough.

I visit the cemetery in San Diego every time I go. My father and mother usually go with me to bring me up to date. It seems the proper thing to do, to go to pay my respects to the people there that I love so much: My grandmother, Maria. My grandfather, Gonzalo, who died suddenly coming out of the meat market, clutching his package of meat to his chest. They said he was dead before he hit the ground. My uncle Juan, the musician, next to them, dead at thirty-three. My little sister, Belinda, who died needlessly of dysentery, who we baptized with tap water because the priest could not come to the house to give her last rites. My uncle Merce, insane, but generous and kind, who used to curse everyone in town, who knew everyone's birthday. Next to him Adolfo, his brother, buried in name only since shortly after buying his tombstone he was kidnapped from San Diego as a mindless old man by someone who claimed to be his illegitimate son—buried in San Antonio. My great-grandfather, who lived almost one hundred years, who spent a week in agony before he died while we played marbles outside his window. My aunt Pepa, the crazy one, who lost all her children in one year. The list goes on. Garcia. Saenz. Gonzalez. Garza. Arguijo. Flores. Everett.

The ringing of the bell never ends.

There is a universality of mankind. There are no bad towns. A little town in south Texas is the same as a little town in John Donne's England where someone also runs to the church to ask for whom the bell tolls.

Some day the bell in San Diego will toll for me. Let the good priest ring it loud and clear. Let the children run to learn my name from the good priest. Let them scatter from the church like summer butterflies, my name on their lips as they run home to pass the word.

As for me, in the end, one realizes that life is made up of priorities. Therefore, I know that I will go in peace. It's not how many books I sell that is important. What is important is what I have written that will survive me. What will fulfill the writer's childhood dream of being eternal?

Lastly, I have found that as great a poet as John Donne was, he was not entirely right. Surely the bell tolls for everyone, but your death does not diminish me. On the contrary, each one of us, in having lived, adds to the soul of everyone else.

Bibliography of Place

ROBERT COMPTON,
Book Editor,
The Dallas Morning News

*T*his list is easy prey for critics. It is not expert. It is woefully incomplete. I had not intended it as an authoritative compilation. It excludes some of my favorite books about Texas. It is, rather, a sampling of some readable writing, fiction and non-fiction, about Texas and Texans and it seems to me to give a good sense of what this unique state and some of its people are about.

I have placed *The Texas Almanac* on this list because I think, as a reference work, it tells more about Texas than any other book I know in its compact size. When outsiders of my acquaintance want to know about Texas, I find the *Almanac* is the perfect start. As a matter of fact, I still discover new things about the state almost every time I pick it up.

There are no J. Frank Dobie books on the list, though when I was growing up I spent pleasurable hours reading *Coronado's Children, Apache Gold and Yaqui Silver* and other of Dobie's romantic folktale collections.

I included no Elmer Kelton books only because I couldn't decide which of his fine novels to list.

I admire the work of Rolando Hinojosa and his fiction about the Rio Grande Valley, and Jan Reid's novel *Deerinwater* (which is real life Wichita Falls) and Stephen Harrigan's *Aransas* for its picture of the Gulf Coast, and Carolyn Osborn's short stories, and ... the list goes on and on. But the editor told me there was a limit.

Splendora, by Edward Swift (Viking, 1978).

> Edward Swift, now and for some years a New Yorker, wrote this satirical fiction about a small East Texas town with a knowing eye for its inhabitants. A native of Woodville, Swift penned a fine comic novel with authentically quirky charactersand settings. There's some exaggeration, but it's small town East Texas to the core.

Rafting the Brazos, by Walter McDonald (University of North Texas Press, 1988).

> A poet of national stature, Walter McDonald beautifully captures the landscape of Texas in his writing, and this volume is one of his very best.

The Gay Place, by William Brammer (Houghton Mifflin 1961).

> Brammer's only published novel has been highly praised since it first appeared, and it is still the best portrait of an old-school Texas politician.

Farther Off From Heaven, by William Humphrey (Knopf, 1977).

> Humphrey is one of Texas's most respected writers and the author of a number of fine novels. This is a memoir, wonderfully descriptive of life in East Texas in the 1930s.

A Cold Mind, by David Lindsey (Harper & Row, 1983).

> David Lindsey's first "big" book is set in contemporary Houston and it describes the uniquely Texas metropolis to a "T." Ostensibly a mystery, it is much more—a survey of human depravity, of rich and poor stratas of Houston society, and a physical study of Houston. In following works featuring homicide detective Stuart Haydon, Lindsey continued to use Houston as a setting.

Wanderer Springs, by Robert Flynn (Texas Christian University Press, 1987).

> Flynn draws wonderful pictures of the people and places of near West Texas, the dusty country where he grew up. In this novel, his protagonist reluctantly returns to that country and mixes past tales with the present to beautiful effect.

Time and Place, by Bryan Woolley (Dutton, 1977).

> This story of growing up in Southwest Texas is an exceptionally touching novel by a writer who regrettably no longer writes fiction.

A Personal Country, by A. C. Greene (Knopf, 1969).

> A memoir of the land and the people of the West Texas country around Abilene, where Greene was reared, with fine and strong portraits by a writer who loves and understands his subjects.

The House of Breath, by William Goyen (Random House, 1950).

> The late William Goyen grew up in Trinity in Southeast Texas, and in this, his first novel, his mystical prose focuses on that area. Sense of place was always a strong factor in his later fiction, long after he had left his native state.

The Deer Pasture, by Rick Bass (Texas A&M University Press, 1985).

> Bass, a native of Houston, is one of the nation's most promising young writers. This non-fiction account of some land in Mason County where four generations of Bass men go on deer hunts each year is a sparkling account of family and place.

The Path to Power, by Robert Caro (Harper & Row, 1982).

> Caro drew the ire of Texans in this first volume of a multi-volume biography of Lyndon Johnson, and dodged even more brickbats for the second book of the series. Though he might have misunderstood Texas politics, non-Texan Caro understands writing, and his description of the Hill Country of Johnson's boyhood is an exceptional part of this volume.

Paper Lion, by Leon Hale (Shearer Press, 1986).

> Hale has drawn praise for his fiction and his non-fiction, but this autobiographical piece that was little noticed when published contains some of his strongest writing, and its picture of a family moving from place to place in Texas is an excellent picture of the state in the 1930s.

The Last Picture Show, by Larry McMurtry (Dial Press, 1966).

> Well, perhaps it's not McMurtry's best novel, or even one of his best three, as critics look at it. But it does wonderfully capture a small North Texas town and its people in the 1940s.

The Train to Estelline, by Jane Roberts Wood (Ellen Temple Publishing, 1989).

> This small volume won a popular audience when it was published. Its warm and friendly story of a turn-of-the-century schoolteacher thrust into the harsh life of a West Texas ranch is true to life.

Goodbye to a River, by John Graves (Knopf, 1960).

> A true classic. Graves' story of his boat trip down a pristine stretch of the Brazos River before dams were scheduled to be built is a masterful account of the land, the people along the river, river history, and Graves' personal thoughts as he travels.

Blood and Money, by Tommy Thompson (Doubleday, 1976).

> It's not literature, but it's fine journalism. Thompson's nonfiction account of a rich Houston family and murder and revenge set the standard for future books of its kind. And it made Texas a particularly promising place to look for such stories.

Watt Matthews of Lambshead, by Laura Wilson (Texas State Historical Association, 1989).

> Laura Wilson's startlingly beautiful photography and her simple, concise writing make this one of the very best picture books about Texas. Her story of the Lambshead Ranch and its head man, Watt Matthews—who still supervises its operations—is a perfect portrait of a fading way of life.

Warning: Writer at Work. The Best Collectibles of Larry L. King (Texas Christian University Press, 1985).

> Larry King has been a newspaperman, a magazine writer, a playwright, most often writing of things Texan. He is, probably, and deservedly, the best known Texas journalist on the national scene. This excellent collection draws from much of King's previously published writing.

The Super-Americans, by John Bainbridge (Holt, Rinehart & Winston, 1961).

> Bainbridge's book is a wonderful look at how the rest of the nation perceived 1950s Texas as the land of the big rich oil

and cattle barons, the irresponsible, show-off spenders. If that image was intentionally overblown, most Texans perversely enjoyed it. The portrait stuck for many years, and its vestiges hang on.

Confessions of a Washed-Up Sportswriter, by Gary Cartwright (Texas Monthly Press, 1982).

Another top-notch journalist, Cartwright is eminently readable, and like Larry L. King, dead-on in his colorful writing about the inhabitants of Texas, from cowboys to criminals to sports and athletes.

The Texas Almanac (*The Dallas Morning News*, 1990-91).

A veritable treasure trove of history, geography, government, weather, all kinds of statistical information about the state, with maps and charts.

Contributors

FRANCIS EDWARD ABERNETHY is Professor of English at Stephen F. Austin State University, the Executive Secretary and Editor of the Texas Folklore Society, and a member of the Texas Institute of Letters. Dr. Abernethy attended Stephen F. Austin State University and Louisiana State University, where he received his doctorate in Renaissance Literature. He has taught at Woodville High School, Louisiana State University, Lamar State University, and Stephen F. Austin State University. He is the editor of *Tales From the Big Thicket*, *Built in Texas*, *Legendary Ladies of Texas*, *Folk Art in Texas*, and ten other volumes for the Texas Folklore Society. He has published poetry, short stories, a folk music book entitled *Singin' Texas*, and a book of legends entitled *Legends of Texas' Heroic Age*. He has lectured widely, both popularly and academically. He plays the bass fiddle in the East Texas String Ensemble of Nacogdoches.

Presently director of Texas Christian University Press, JUDY ALTER was for many years a free lance writer and is the author of six novels, four of which are for young adults. Her novel, *Luke and the Van Zandt County War* (1984) was chosen as the Best Juvenile of the Year by the Texas Institute of Letters and *Mattie* (1987) won a Spur Award from Western Writers of America as the Best Western of 1987.

In the spring of 1986, she wrote *So Far From Paradise*, a novel commissioned as a sesquincnetennial project by the *Fort Worth Star-Telegram*. Her most recent works are a critical study of Texas novelist Elmer Kelton—*Elmer Kelton and West Texas: A Literary Relationship* published by the University of North Texas Press—and three young adult novels, *Maggie and Devildust*, *Maggie and the Search for Devildust*, and *Maggie and Devildust—Ridin' High!* will complete the series published by E-Heart and Ellen Temple Publishers of Texas. She is also the author of several books in the First Book Series from Franklin Watts Company: *Growing Up in the Old West*, *Women and the Old West*, *Eli Whitney*, and a forthcoming volume on the Comanches.

DUANE BIDWELL has explored the Oregon Trail, meditated in Thailand and written for an environmental agency in Washington, D.C. He and his wife live in a 70-year-old house on Fort Worth's South Side, but escape to the mountains at every opportunity. In 1990, Bidwell taught for three months at the Times Centre for Media Studies in New Delhi, India, and also led a writing seminar for the Dalai Lama's public-relations staff. He was a reporter for the *Fort Worth Star-Telegram* and is working on a manuscript about his experiences in Thailand.

TONY CLARK's poems and stories have appeared in a number of publications. His poems have been collected in three books: *Llano Sons: 3 from the Southwest* and *Llano Sons: Trips and Passings* with coauthors Jim Harris and John Garmon, and his solo collection *Fate 1 Mile*. He has twice won the Boswell Poetry Prize, and his writings also have received awards from the Poetry Society of Texas, *Southwest Heritage*, Texas Christian University, and the Fort Worth Art Museum. A native of Jacksboro, Texas, Clark taught English at Paris Junior College for nineteen years before moving to Arizona in 1990. He currently teaches writing at Scottsdale Community College.

BETSY COLQUITT teaches at TCU and has published poems over several years, including a poetry collection titled *HONOR CARD*. In 1965 she received the faculty recognition award from students in the honors program for outstanding contribution to the intellectual life of TCU. In 1982 Betsy received the first Chancellor's Award for Teaching.

ROBERT COMPTON, book editor of *The Dallas Morning News*, is a fifth-generation Texan, a native of Teague, Freestone County. He attended Texas A&M University in 1944, interrupted college to serve in the U.S. Navy during World War II, and finished his formal education at Southern Methodist University. He was a newspaper reporter in Pampa and later in Garland, where he edited a bi-weekly newspaper for five years before joining *The Dallas Morning News* in 1956. After serving in a variety of writing and editing positions at *The News*, he became editor of its Books pages in 1978.

PAUL K. CONNER, JR. is a 61-year-old practitioner of internal medicine in Dallas, Texas, where he has practiced for thirty plus years. He lives in North Dallas with his wife, Janie, and has two children, Casey, who lives in Dallas, and, Kelley who teaches school in Melbourne, Australia. Paul Conner was reared in Jacksboro, Texas and took his undergraduate degree at SMU and medical degree at Baylor Medical College in Houston, Texas. His post-graduate training was in Houston, Ann Arbor, and Parkland Hospital in Dallas. His career has spanned the "horse-and-buggy days" of medical practice as he remembers from his youth to the present high-tech approach to medicine. He actually feels more effective somewhere in between the two extremes.

NEIL DANIEL, a native of Minnesota, has lived in Texas for over forty years and in the neighborhood he calls home for some fifteen. Active in the neighborhood organization, he writes musicals about neighborhood life, edits the newsletter from time to time, and conducts workshops on neighborhood organization. His essays on urban life have appeared in the *Fort Worth Magazine*, the *Fort Worth Star-Telegram*, and other city publications. Daniel teaches English at Texas Christian University. His academic interests include composition theory, comprehensive writing programs, and English literature before 1500. His most recent book is a *Guide to Style and Mechanics*.

EVERETT FLY was born and raised in San Antonio, Texas, where he presently resides. After attending the University of Texas at Austin and graduating with a Bachelor of Architecture, he entered the Harvard University Graduate School of Design to study Landscape Architecture. When he graduated, he became the first black American to earn the MLA from Harvard. He has taught architecture at the University of Texas at Austin and conducted seminars and studios in historic preservation at the University of California at Berkeley and Texas A&M University.

He has been responsible for various special projects, including the Nicodemus, Kansas Historic American Building Survey Project; Black Dallas Remembered; International Boulevard Downtown Urban Design Team at Atlanta, Georgia; "America by Design," as a panel member for a 5-part PBS series; Eatonville, Florida Historic Resources Survey. In addition, he has served on the Board of Review for the National Register of Historic places, Texas; the City of San Antonio Board of Review for Historic Districts and Landmarks; Texas Committee for the Humanities. He is now Chairman of TCH. He is also a registered landscape architect (Texas, California, Georgia, Alabama, Florida) and a registered architect (Texas, California, Florida).

ROBERT FLYNN is novelist in residence at Trinity University. A native Texan, he is the author of four novels, *North to Yesterday, In the House of the Lord, The Sounds of Rescue, The Signs of Hope*, and *Wanderer Springs*. His dramatic adaptation of Faulkner's *As I Lay Dying* was the United States entry at the Theater of Nations in Paris in 1964 and won a Special Jury Award. He is also the author of a two-part documentary, "A Cowboy Legacy," shown on ABC-TV, a collection of short stories, *Seasonal Rain*, and a nonfiction narrative, *A Personal War in Vietnam*.

Flynn has won awards from the Texas Institute of Letters and the National Cowboy Hall of Fame. His novel *North to Yesterday* was named one of the Best Books of the Year by the *New York Times*, and his collection of stories was co-winner of the Texas Literary Festival Award. His books have been translated into German, Spanish, Dutch, Afrikaans, Malayalam, Arabic, Tamil, Hindi, Kanada, and Vietnamese. Flynn is a member of the Texas Institute of Letters, The Authors Guild, The Writers Guild of America, and P.E.N.

LIONEL GARCIA was born in San Diego, Texas, on August 20th, 1935, one of four children. He has been writing since the early fifties. Almost all of his writings have dealt with Mexican-American life in the United States. In 1983 he won the Discovery Prize from PEN Southwest for his novel, *Leaving Home*, published in 1985 through a grant from the National Endowment for the Arts and Texas Commission for the Arts. His short stories, "The Wedding," "The Day They Took My Uncle," "Some People Are That Way," "The Sergeant," "The Apparition," "Tutoring Amnesty," have all appeared in various anthologies and literary magazines.

His second novel. *A Shroud in the Family,* was released in the spring of 1987. Currently he is working on a new novel, a collection of short stories and a play. He is married to Noemi

Barrera Garcia and has three children: a daughter, Rose, and two sons, Carlos and Paul. By day he is a Veterinarian in Seabrook, Texas, a suburb south of Houston.

JIM HARRIS is a poet, a teacher, a folklorist and a scholar. Presently, he is Professor of English at New Mexico Junior College in Hobbs, New Mexico. He was named New Mexico Eminent Scholar in 1989 and Distinguished Alumnus, East Texas State University in 1988. A past president of the Texas Folklore Society, Jim is a photographer, operates Hawk Press, contributes to publications through reviews, criticism, poetry, fiction and interviews. Jim's wife, Mary, and his son, Hawk, share the culture, flavor and life of the Southwest.

FRANCES MAYHUGH HOLDEN earned a BA in anthropology and an MA in history from Texas Tech. She holds memberships and offices in numerous arts and humanities organizations including an appointment by the governor to the Texas Commission on the Arts from 1966 to 1975. Her chairmanships include the Ranching Heritage Center and the Ranching Heritage Association. Frances has been acting director for the museum at Texas Tech, assistant to the museum director for exhibits, educational and public relations, and researcher for the fresco mural of the South Plains. In addition, she researched, collected for and established the Art of the Southwest for the museum's permanent art collection, coordinated and served on the executive committee for the West Texas Museum Association, founded and coordinated the Women's Council for the West Texas Museum Association. She has been a guest lecturer and instructor in geography at Texas Tech and research associate for history. She and her husband, Curry, live in an adobe house which they built.

ELMER KELTON is the author of 30 novels, published over about 35 years. The latest are *The Man Who Rode Midnight, Dark Thicket, Stand Proud, The Wolf and the Buffalo, Eyes of the Hawk*, and *Sons of Texas* series published under the pseudonym Tom Early. *Honor at Daybreak* was published in 1991. Three of his novels have appeared in *Reader's Digest Condensed Books*. Three-times winner of the Western Heritage Award from the

National Cowboy Hall of Fame, for *The Time It Never Rained, The Good Old Boys* and *The Man Who Rode Midnight*. Four-time winner of the Spur Award from Western Writers of America for *Buffalo Wagons, The Day the Cowboys Quit, The Time It Never Rained,* and *Eyes of the Hawk*. In 1987 he received the Barbara McCombs/Lon Tinkle Award for "continuing excellence in Texas letters" from the Texas Institute of Letters. In 1990 he received the Distinguished Achievement Award from the Western Literature Association.

Alabama-born JAMES WARD LEE has lived in Texas since 1948, which, he says now makes him a native. He is chairman of the English Department and Director of the Center for Texas Studies at the University of North Texas. Best known as a folklorist, editor, and literary critic, Lee is author of many books, articles, and papers. His most recent book is *Classics of Texas Fiction*. He has been editor of the critical quarterly *Studies in the Novel* and the literary magazine *American Literary Review: A National Journal of Poems and Stories*. He is currently editor of *New Texas*, an annual devoted to publishing the best Texas poetry and fiction. Lee is a member of the Texas Institute of Letters and a past president of the Texas Folklore Society. He began writing fiction in "the early part of my late middle age." The story included in this volume is his third published story.

PAUL PATTERSON is a native of Lonesome County, Lonesome, Texas—Pecos, Crane and Sierra Blanca. Eventually he settled down to life in Lonesome Country as a school teacher and writer. As a matter of fact, he was Elmer Kelton's teacher and Kelton gives him credit as an influence which shows up in every piece he writes. In 1946, Paul published a book, a parody, *Sam Magoo and Texas Too*, which was illustrated by Kelton. Paul says he wrote the book to keep himself from losing his mind during World War II while he encountered another kind of lonesome country on a Pacific island. Paul has published *Pecos Tales* and *Crazy Women in the Rafters*—all about time and place. He is a cowboy poet, and is making a comeback, if indeed, he was ever gone, in that old genre of the range which is being revitalized. He presents papers at the Texas Folklore Society every year in the midst of a group who crowd the room to hear him.

MARGARET RAMBIE is currently news editor for the *Uvalde Leader News*. She was born in Oklahoma, spent time in Louisiana as a small child and again in the mid-fifties when "we moved there to keep from starving to death during the drought." She grew up in San Antonio, but moved with her parents to Uvalde in 1950. Margaret has three children and three grandchildren. Her husband, Johnny, owns Foster-Rambie Grass Seed Company which her father founded in 1949. In addition to the *Leader News* her articles have appeared in inflight magazines, other state newspapers and her photos illustrated a *Texas Monthly* story about Joe Newton. She is a member of Texas Press Women and was chosen as that organization's Communicator of Achievement in 1988 and won its contest's sweepstakes award in 1980. Margaret has also won writing awards from Texas Press Association and South Texas Press Association.

CLAY REYNOLDS, Associate Professor of English, Novelist in Residence, and Associate Director of the Center for Texas Studies at the University of North Texas, was born in Quanah, Texas. He has authored more than two hundred scholarly articles, essays, and book reviews, and he has delivered more than fifty papers and lectures to professional associations and learned societies. Reynolds' four published books include two novels, *The Vigil* and *Agatite*; a scholarly study, *Stage Left: The Development of the American Social Drama in the Thirties*, and *Taking Stock: A Larry McMurtry Casebook*, which he edited. He has published articles in national magazines and essay collections and his short fiction has appeared in numerous little magazines as well as in anthologies. Forthcoming works include two new novels, *Franklin's Crossing* and *Texas Augustus*, and a history of the *Southwestern Exposition and Livestock Show*.

JOYCE ROACH grew up in Jacksboro, Texas and has never gotten over it nor does she want to. Her rural roots in ranch country provide much of the substance of her writing in non-fiction, fiction, humorous narrative, musical folk drama and children's stories. A member of the Texas Institute of Letters and member and past president of the Texas Folklore Society, she is also a three-time winner of the Spur Award from Western Writers of America, one for *The Cowgirls* published by the University of North Texas Press, and is the winner of the Carr P. Collins award for non-fiction from TIL for a book co-authored with Ernestine Sewell. She is a member of the Texas State Historical Association and board member of the Texas Alliance for the Humanities.

JAN EPTON SEALE lives in the Rio Grande Valley of Texas. Her short stories have been published in such places as *The Chicago Tribune, Newsday,* and *The San Francisco Chronicle* through PEN Syndicated Fiction Projects and in journals such as *Concho River Review, New Mexico Humanities Review,* and *Yale Review.* The publication of a short story collection, *Airlift,* is forthcoming. Articles and poems have appeared in periodicals such as *Texas Monthly* and *Nimrod.* She is the author of two books of poetry, *Bonds* and *Sharing the House* and is one of four poets featured in *Texas Poets in Concert: A Quartet* published by the University of North Texas Press. In 1982 Seale held a creative writing fellowship through the National Endowment of the Arts.

Writer and teacher, TIM SEIBLES is a 1977 graduate of Southern Methodist University and an MFA graduate of the Writing Program at Vermont College on Mt. Pelier. In January of 1990 he was awarded a NEA fellowship grant for literature. He has taught English for ten years, eight of which were spent at North Dallas High School, and two at the Episcopal School of Dallas. Tim's first full-length book of poetry, *Body Moves* was published in June of 1988 and went into a second printing last year. He is also the author of two chapbook ballads that are illustrated by James Sharper. While publishing in regional and national literary journals such as *The Sun, Southwest Review, Bloomsbury Review,* and *Black American Literature Forum,* he was twice voted "Best Local Writer or Poet" ('86 & '89) by the *Dallas Observer* readers' poll. Currently, Tim has just completed his second full-length poetry manuscript and continues to work on *Bottom Dollar,* his first novel.

ERNESTINE SEWELL is a former professor at the University of Texas at Arlington and has published widely on topics ranging from education to linguistics and from modern literature to

Southwest life, literature, and lore. She is co-author of *Eats: A Folk History of Texas Foods* which won the Carr P. Collins Award from the Texas Institute of Letters in 1989. Ernestine and her husband, Charles Linck, live in Commerce where both are active in the Texas Folklore Society, East Texas Historical Association and the Texas State Historical Association. They travel, write, speak and publish books on their own press, Cow Hill Press.

Born on the banks of Dreary Hollow in Llano County, ERNEST B. SPECK has taught English in four southwestern states, including three colleges in Texas. He has also worked in journalism in Chicago and Paris, France. In addition to assorted works, chiefly in folklore-folklife, he has published *Mody C. Boatright*, Southwest Writers Series, 1971; *Mody Boatright, Folklorist*, editor, 1973; *Benjamin Capps*, Western Writers Series, 1981; and *An Assortment of Effusions*, (verse), 1989. Now retired, he lives alone and licks his wounds.

Named the official Cowboy Poet of Texas by the Texas Legislature in 1991, RED STEAGALL's career has covered a period of twenty-five years and spanned the globe from Australia to the Middle East. He has performed for heads of state including a special party for President Reagan at the White House and for government officials in eight Middle Eastern countries. Red has had careers in agricultural chemistry in Texas, the music industry in Hollywood, California, and has spent the last twelve years as a recording artist, songwriter, and television and motion picture personality. Although Red is best known for his Texas Swing dance music, he is beloved by Texas cowboys for the quiet times they have spent with him around chuck wagon campfires.

M. JANE YOUNG joined the faculty of the American Studies Department of the University of New Mexico as an Associate Professor in the fall of 1987. Prior to that time she taught for five years in the Program of Folklore and Ethnomusicology at the University of Texas at Austin. Her interests include: material culture and ethnoaesthetics, landscape studies, Native American folklore and linguistics, museum studies, gender studies, and ethnoastronomy. She has conducted extensive fieldwork at the Pueblo of Zuni in New Mexico where she produced a traveling exhibit of rock art of the Zuni-Cibola region in conjunction with the tribal museum committee. She has served on folk art museum panels for both the Texas Commission on the Arts and NEH. Her book, *Signs from the Ancestors: Zuni Culture Symbolism and Perceptions of Rock Art*, which focuses on the verbal and visual traditions of the Zunis, was published in 1988.